Don't Look Back

Don't Look Back

Bridget Cassidy

Pentland Press, Inc.
England·USA·Scotland

PUBLISHED BY PENTLAND PRESS, INC.
5122 Bur Oak Circle, Raleigh, North Carolina 27612
United States of America
(919)782-0281

ISBN: 1-57197-133-5
Library of Congress Catalog Card Number 98-067427

Printed in the United States of America

In memory of my dear friend
Bridget McGovern Lynch
Bryn Mawr, Pennsylvania
Formerly of Owencham
Corlough
County Cavan
Ireland

Table of Contents

CHAPTER 1
The Beginning *1*

CHAPTER 2
Bridget in Ireland *13*

CHAPTER 3
Home Again *27*

CHAPTER 4
Wake Up Call for Da *51*

CHAPTER 5
Bridget Growing Up *67*

CHAPTER 6
Bridget Looks Ahead to America *91*

Acknowledgments

I would like to offer special thanks to my son, Mike, who loves my story. My old friend Marcella DeLoria, who took wonderful photographs of Govan for my book. Effie McMillen, Elder Park Library. Veronica Cunnigham, Secretary, Govan Heritage Trail. And my new friend Nancy Blackburn, who helped Mike edit my story.

"A Proud Wee Govanite"

Here's to my parents,
Their memory I treasure.
They taught me the values,
I've tried hard to measure.
And to dear old Govan,
Where I learned about life,
Be kind to your neighbor,
Don't get too galice,
And try to be nice.
Always clean and neat.
Stand on my own two feet.
To depend on myself,
Not everybody else.
I've traveled far and wide,
Met people of every kind,
Have friends I love dearly,
But believe your's sincerely,
I have always been so clearly,
A proud wee Govanite.

-Bridget Cassidy

CHAPTER 1

The Beginning

Our crowded tenement building, standing in the Govan district of Glasgow, Scotland, was one of hundreds of dreary-looking, black-smoked three-story buildings. The building was home to fifteen families crammed into flats, with five flats on each floor or landing, and a spiral, railed, cement stairway leading up to them. Our entire family lived directly above McColls' bar—Mom, Dad, and five children. We were known as "The Dowd Family."

The Harmony Bar in the Govan district of Glasgow, Scotland.

My dad, Eddy, was an Irishman who came to work in Scotland in 1939. He joined two of his brothers, John and Martin, who had previously came over from Co Sligo in Ireland. Work was plentiful in those days, and as land-working farmers from Ireland, these three young men were not afraid to work long hours in Glasgow. Dad was a smooth-talking, charming lad of twenty-seven, very handsome, with dark blue eyes and a mop of wavy, brown hair. He had a nice Irish accent.

Govan District

My mom, Rosetta Hamilton, a slim, pretty, dark-haired, brown-eyed lassie of nineteen, met Dad at an Irish dance hall, and it was love at first sight. After keeping company with Eddy for a few months, Mom became pregnant. When she was five months along expecting me, Dad did the "decent thing" and married her in the Catholic church. However, the priest informed them that they could not be married at the altar, so the marriage ceremony was performed in the vestry room instead.

Mom's parents were unhappy with the marriage, as they were not too keen on Eddy, to say the least. When he was sober he was polite, but whenever he was intoxicated he became more changeable than the Scottish weather. On top of this, Eddy enjoyed gambling on the horse races. Sometimes he won, but mostly he LOST!

Her parents, my Granda Andrew and "Maw" Elizabeth Hamilton, were from Northern Ireland. They had come to Scotland to be married because of religious reasons—Granda being a Protestant and "Maw" Catholic. However my mom and her two sisters and four brothers were brought up in the Catholic faith. I vaguely remember Granda as a tall, quiet man with snow white hair. Grandma was small brunette. She kept two boarders in her already crowded home. Unlike our tenement,

Grandma's had two bedrooms, a big kitchen, a bathroom, and a long hallway. My mom told me Granda would kick her behind all the way down this hallway when she was late coming home from a dance or visiting with her many friends—which was often, since she was so popular and good natured.

Mom left school at age fourteen, as that was school-leaving age in her day. She soon went to work in the restaurant beside her home. Morgan's was a well-known eating place because it served delicious meals to the customers at reasonable prices. One time she got her sister Nora a job there. The very first day that Mom was training her, she told Nora, "Put salt in the soup." Unbeknownst to Mom, Nora proceeded to pour the entire bag of salt into the big soup pot! Nobody noticed until the noon dinner-time rush, when the customers had a fit over "salt soup."

I was born in April 1940 at the local Southern General Hospital. My parents had me christened two weeks later and named me Bridget, after my dad's mother, Bridget Dowd in Ireland. My mom, however, thought this name sounded too Irish, so I was nicknamed "Beatrice," which was supposed to be a variation of the name Bridget. In 1942, my brother Edward was born, and in 1944 we had a new baby sister who was named Rosetta after mom, and called Rose for short.

Saint Anthony's Presbytery

When I was almost five years old, I played on the stairs of our building and outside at the back, where the trash cans were kept. The metal trash cans were usually spilling over with trash, coal, ashes, newspapers, and kitty poop. A common occupation for us tenement children was "Raking the Middens," which meant searching through the cans looking for comic books. These middens were enclosed by brick alcoves, and my friends and I soon learned to climb up to the top of their roofs. They were not really very high, maybe five feet tall. One day when Mom was busy caring for my sister Rose, my brother Ed also came to play, and as children will do, he attempted to follow me and began climbing up the middens behind me. Dad appeared on the scene and yelled, "Come down immediately!" I hesitated too long, and when I finally descended, he slapped me with the back of his hand all the way home. After this episode, there was no more midden climbing until years later.

When I was five it was time to attend St. Anthony's School, and I loved it. I had such a fun time. There were lots of story books, coloring books, and crayons—plus a wonderful teacher to fuss over me and all the girls and boys in my classroom. She taught us our ABCs and how to count, and read us some wonderful stories.

One day when school was closed for a holy day, I went out to the middens and began rummaging through the trash cans, trying to find comic books. A neighbor boy called out to me from his upstairs back window, "What are you looking for?"

"Comics," I replied.

"I have plenty of comic books up here," and he invited me to come up to his place to look at them. I did not know the boy very well, as he was part of a large family, and was at least seventeen or eighteen years old. When I reached his flat, he sexually molested me. As he coaxed me to lay on top of the bed with my legs spread and my pants removed, he rubbed his penis up and down my vagina. Luckily for me, his brother returned home from school and began yelling, "What are you doing?" While they argued, I got up off the bed and slipped silently out the door, unnoticed, and ran home to Mom.

When I reached home, Mom was in the kitchen bathing my brother Ed in a basin of water. I must have pointed out that his birdie was tiny compared to the neighbor boy's. All hell broke loose. She grabbed me by the hand and marched me to the boy's door. She hammered loudly on the door, and when he opened it, she screamed and punched him in the face and head until he finally managed to close the door. That night Mom escorted me to the police station. There I was examined by a female officer, who shone a bright light between my legs. I could not understand what all the fuss was about.

The next day when the boy's mother met my Mom, she said, "You did not have to do that to my son."

Mom yelled back, "No, I should have murdered the swine!"

The boy joined a branch of the service and I never saw him again.

I recall a very exciting time when the Second World War ended. When Mom's brother, Marcus, came home from Germany, everyone was singing and dancing in the streets, and all of the children were playing with the discarded gas masks and army helmets. We had sing-a-longs around the back court, the back yard of our tenement buildings, and everyone rejoiced. Although it was a happy time for the men who returned home, I was too young to realize that an awful lot of dads, husbands, and sweethearts never did make it home because they were killed in action.

Uncle Marcus presented me with a sixpenny silver bit which I promptly put in my mouth and swallowed. Mom forced me to take castor-oil laxative and then waited anxiously for nature to take its course. Sure enough, the next day I was absolutely mesmerized at the sight of the shiny sixpence gleaming in my poop.

My aunt Nora, the same aunt who accidentally made "salt soup," had a sailor boyfriend named Bill Wiltshire, an Englishman who actually came from Wiltshire. He was fond of me and gave me a yo-yo that totally delighted me as it jumped up and down on its string. When two men, Bill and another serviceman, proposed marriage to her, she chose to marry Bill. They were very much in love.

Mom's other sister, Lilly, a stylish, pretty woman, also married her sailor boyfriend. He was a very good-looking Scot named Jimmy Curren, although I didn't think him quite as handsome as Uncle Bill.

My uncle Marcus was dating Mom's friend, Annie Gaitons, who had the most gorgeous, long, naturally-curling

Patsy and Violet outside the shop on their street.

hair. She was a pretty woman, who would sing songs to my brother Ed, sister Rose, and me when they baby sat us. They married eventually.

Some of Mom's lady friends wore leg tan, a tan-colored liquid which they rubbed over their legs to make it appear like they were wearing nylon stockings. Nylon stockings were a genuine prize for a girl to obtain, as they were scarce and also expensive.

We got a boarder, an Englishman named Mr. Nelson, who was employed at the Fairfield shipyard only a short distance from our house. He enjoyed living with us, but his hobby was playing the accordion while sitting at an open window. This drove my parents, especially my dad, crazy in a short period of time, so Mr. Nelson did not stay too long with us.

Offices of Kvaerner Govan Ltd., originally Fairfield Shipyard offices.

One Saturday morning he took me to the shoe store and let me choose a new pair of shoes that were advertised in the window display. They were black, patent leather with ankle straps and buttons. They were so shiny. I really missed him when he left.

On our street stood two brick air-raid shelters, where some of the neighbors ran whenever the sirens went off during the war. We children only played around them on the outside, because they were pitch black dark inside. We all kept "the blackout," with our windows covered with dark blinds to ensure that no lights could be seen by the enemy's night-raiding bombers. Yet, despite these precautions, places in Scotland were bombed, especially Dumbarton and Clydebamk. Even a part of

Linthouse, less than a mile away from my home, received some of Hitler's fury. The McLoy family was wiped out. I often overheard my parents and their friends sadly discussing the loss of so many women, babies and children.

Our tenement was surrounded by small shops, and Mom often sent me to the one right next to us that was run by our neighbors. They sold bread, cereal, canned food, soap, laundry detergent, and assorted items. Mom would give me a list to hand to the assistant and I was to remind them to mark the items in their credit book until my dad got paid. This was called "tick for credit," and on Fridays we paid the bill. Mom would get so mad at me because whenever she sent me to this shop, I would wait until I was down in the street and then start yelling, "Ma, Ma. Is it on tick?" She would appear at the window and nod her head yes and also shake her fist at me.

Foods like sugar, butter, and eggs were scarce, and everyone had ration books. When we used up our ration allotment of sugar, Ma simply used a piece of dry bread to rub out the mark and sent me to get more. If one of the rationed eggs was rotten when it was cracked, I was sent back to the shop with it in a cup. The assistant would hold her nose and say, "How many?"

I usually replied, "Two or three," knowing she would not even bother to check it, the smell was so foul.

When I was five, Mom got a job as a lamplighter. Everyone in the tenements had electricity, but the outside landings were gas lit. She went out at dusk with a long pole shaped like a walking cane and reached up to light the street lamps. She would then return in the early morning to extinguish them. The job was scary, as she had to step over drunks on the stairs on Friday nights occasionally, and she was even propositioned one time. Needless to say, she only had this job for a short time.

Later, Mom got a night-shift job working for a fish company, packing kipper herring. Although they supplied her with a rubber apron to wear, the smell was difficult to wash off, and she always reeked of fish. We ate lots of fish, since her boss often presented her with a wooden box filled with them, and she would give the neighbors whatever was leftover. Dad also worked the night shift, so we got a sitter to stay overnight with us until they returned early the following morning. Our sitter was named Irene Spence, a neighbor girl whom we dearly loved. My dad said her long hair was like acorn, the color so lovely.

On 16 March 1946, we got a new baby sister. Since she arrived the day before St. Patrick's Day, my parents named her Patricia and gave her a middle name of Mary, taken from Mary McNally, a close friend of Mom's. Patsy, as we all came to know her, had delicate features, a thin face and dark brown eyes. She rapidly became a "mommy's girl" and was crazy about Ma. She was the image of Ma, too.

We children enjoyed summertime. The Elder Park, a block away, was a delightful place for us to play, with beautiful flowers and rose-bushes, a pond filled with tiny fish, a swing park, and a sand patch we called "The Sandy Hole." There was also a maypole swing with rope, which I did not enjoy because I always hit my head off the pole. We would take along a bottle of lemonade, and Ed, Rose, and I took turns drinking it until it was gone. Our only concern at the park was the park keeper, who was nick-named "The Parky." He had a very important job and was kept overly busy with so many chil-dren to keep his eye on. He had a whistle, which hung around his neck, and if anyone stepped too near any of the flowers, he was not shy at using it.

Govan Old Parrish Church.

In June we had "The Old Govan Fair" parade, with bands, clowns, and men riding "Penny Farthing Bikes." These unique contraptions had a huge wheel in front and a small wheel on the back. The fair was a grand event, and the Govan Road sidewalks were filled with happy spectators. Little children could be seen waving tiny flags and balloons in the summer air. The windows of the buildings were all opened wide, so row upon row of neighbors would peer out into the street to view the parade as it passed by.

Halloween was a fun time. Dad bought apples for us and put them into a basin of cold water. We would stick our head in and try to catch an apple with our teeth. He called this "duckin' for apples." Children dressed themselves in grown-up clothing, usually their mom's high heel shoes and an old dress or the boys would borrow Dad's pants, shirt, jacket, tie, and a hat or work cap called a "bunnet." We would parade around our neighbors' homes begging for treats and saying, "I will sing and dance The Highland Fling, if you will give something for Halloween." We went in groups and usually got pennies or apples. Since Halloween was always held on a Friday, occasionally we would meet tipsy neighbors who would give us a few silver coins.

The following day we ran to the sweet shop to buy goodies, where the window and shelves were stacked with tall jars of assorted treats—Bon Bons, jellybeans, Gob Stoppers, Cinnamon Stix, and Lucky Dip. Our next stop was a penny soda-pop shop where we stood at the counter because there were no seats or stools. The elderly owner, Miss Fiddler, gave glasses of pop filled to the brim. She knew all our names and would always inquire, "How's your mom getting along?" In fact, all the shopkeepers were polite and friendly in this respect.

Christmas and New Years were big-time holidays. Mom was a good cook and baker, and she would make us rhubarb dumplings and raisin cake. Dad saved money to purchase whisky and sherry wine, and he insisted on giving the mailman a good shot for the holidays. We children scribbled letters to Santa Claus and put them up the chimney and hoped they didn't burn up in the coal fireplace. I always wanted a doll that could say "Mama" and open and close its eyes, but with so many children in the family, we gladly accepted whatever presents Santa left for us. Although our stockings were filled with comics, sweets, apples, an orange, and a few trinkets, I never did get my doll.

My grandparents from Ireland usually sent our family a goose or a turkey for Christmas Day. The local butcher kept it for us in his walk-in freezer until Mom was ready to cook it. He did not charge her anything because she was a steady customer and bought meat from his shop: sausages, bacon, stewing chops, and beef burger. Mom made a delicious, big pot of Scotch broth every Saturday night using a piece of beef with bone in it. The soup lasted the entire week, and Mom told us it was good for us because it would stick to our ribs. Of course, we never questioned this remark—Mom was always right!

On Christmas Eve, Mom cooked the bird and then my parents attended midnight mass. This was the only time Mom attended mass, except for maybe a wedding or funeral. Her brother and his wife, our uncle Robert and aunt Maggy, visited after the midnight service, as there was plenty of food left from dinner. Christmas and New Years were the only times we ate so well.

The excitement of the coming New Year meant everything in our flat had to be spotless. Every two years Dad papered and painted our only bedroom, the hallway and kitchen, and finally the small toilet room. Although he complained the entire time, he did a fantastic job. He was a handyman and scraped, grained, and varnished the doors to the flat like a professional painter.

New Year's Eve, or "Hogmany," as it is called in Scotland, was a grand time indeed and everyone was extremely happy. At twelve midnight the church bell chimes rang out, the shipyard whistle tooted, and any boats on the river Clyde blew their whistles. Then the party began. Friends visited each other's homes, and party goers brought along the customary bottle of liquor. The first person to arrive was called "The First Foot," meaning the first person to enter the home after midnight. It was also understood that anyone with red hair must be polite enough to arrive later, since red hair was considered unlucky. We children were fed fruits, cheese, and non-alcoholic wine, and then we turned into bed exhausted. At this early age we were too young to

River Clyde

remember all the loved ones who never enjoyed another New Year's because the war had taken their lives.

Once a year, on "Shrove Tuesday," the day before Ash Wednesday, Mom made pancakes that all enjoyed. The pancakes were as large as the skillet, and we slathered them with margarine and jam and gobbled them up rather quickly.

In 1947 it seemed to me that many people were catching tuberculosis, scarlet fever, and whooping cough. I remember Uncle Tommy Hamilton's wife, my aunt Roseann Reardon, contracted tuberculosis.

She was a lovely, delicate woman who had at least four children—our cousins—Tommy, Jimmy, Betty, and the baby Maureen. They lived in tenements on Water Row, close to the river Clyde, across from the Govan Cross underground subway. The living conditions were not good there, and Aunt Roseann died shortly after Cousin Maureen was born.

My aunt Lilly and uncle Jimmy returned from England and came to live with Gran Hamilton. I had two new cousins whom I had never met—Betty, who was about my age, and Billy, who was my brother Ed's age—and I liked them both immediately.

Gran preferred that we call her "Maw," as she said calling her "Gran" made her feel old. One day when visiting Maw, we found a new arrival. A little, thin, smiling, pretty child stood gazing up curiously at us. She was our cousin Maureen Hamilton, Aunt Roseann's baby daughter. Granmaw was raising her in her already crowded home.

Granda Andrew was not to be seen, and I assumed he was at work. However, I soon learned that he had died. Apparently, he and Maw were very happy together, and his pet name for her was, "my lovely, black-haired Bess." Granmaw remained a recluse for the rest of her life, mourning over his death. She had lots of friends who visited her, plus all of us grandchildren. Two of Maw's close friends were Mrs. Baird and Carri McCann. My granmaw was a good cook and laundress, and she did the boarders' laundry too. In the bathroom was a cast-iron bathtub, toilet, and a mangle wringer—a gadget with rollers and a handle to turn them to wring the water out of the wet clothing. She hung the clothes to dry on a wooden pulley also in the bathroom. Our pulley was in the kitchen, as this was where most people hung wet clothing so the heat from the fireplace could dry them faster. Gran's home held a coal bunker in the hallway where the coal-delivery man deposited bags of coal weekly. All of the tenements had "coal bunkers," as they were called.

CHAPTER 2

Bridget in Ireland

I contracted the whooping cough so badly that our family doctor advised my parents to send me to the countryside for fresh air, away from the smoking chimneys and smog of Govan. Since my parents did not know anyone who lived in the Scottish countryside, they decided that I should be sent to my grandparents' home in Co Sligo, Ireland. My uncle Marcus volunteered to escort me there.

Bridget, age 7, in Ireland.

We sailed from the Broomilaw dock in Glasgow and traveled overnight to Londonderry in Northern Ireland. I remember that the boat rocked, as the sea was rough, and lots of passengers, including my uncle and I, became seasick. Apparently the Irish Sea is treacherous at the point where it meets the Atlantic Ocean. This area of the world is called "Ailsa Craig," and nicknamed "Patrick's Milestone." Onboard the ship, the passengers sang songs, and I recall *Galway Bay* as being the most popular.

When the boat arrived at Londonderry at 6 AM, my dear uncle and I walked towards the bus station to inquire as to the scheduled time the bus would leave for Sligo. Since it was not leaving until 9 AM, we decided to walk up the road a spell. The smell of cooking bacon soon drew us to a charming cafe where we ate breakfast. I remember Uncle Marcus ate a hearty meal of eggs, bacon, and sausage, while I only had tea and toast because I was whooping and coughing so badly.

We boarded a bus for another long journey, and we slept most of the way. At the times when I was drowsily awake, I remember looking out of the bus's window and seeing miles of open countryside. The hills were dotted with sheep and cows enjoying their morning meals. In some remote areas, children accompanied by adults were standing next to the roadside to see the bus and wave to the passengers. This gave me a warm, welcome feeling, which was much needed after my tumultuous boat ride.

When we finally arrived at our destination, there was a car and driver to meet us. Gran and Granda Dowd lived on a big farm, along with my cousin Nancy and uncle Jimmy. The house was a three-bedroom, white-washed cottage with a black, slated roof. There was a small, man-made, concrete wall around the house, and a concrete pathway led to the front kitchen door. A big open-hearth fireplace stood out to greet us, and the smell of burning turf, used for fuel and heat, was a pleasant and inviting, warm welcome.

Gran was a tiny, stern-looking woman, yet she was pretty, as her eyes were dark blue and her snow white hair was curled at the back of her head. She was dressed in a long, black dress and wore black shoes. Granda was a tall, balding, blue-eyed, kind-looking, handsome man, and he wore a gray jacket, black pants, and boots.

Jimmy was also home from his work in the fields. He was not too tall, maybe five-foot-eight. He was a smiling, good-natured type of man, with blue eyes and nice hair. He was wearing Wellington rubber boots that were turned down at the top. Cousin Nancy was a teenager, an attractive lass, with dark hair and brown eyes, dressed in a skirt and sweater. She had been at Gran's house since she was two years old, when she had caught bronchitis in Govan. My aunt Annie and uncle John had to send her there, as she was not getting well while living in Scotland.

We were made welcome and fed a delicious supper of piping-hot mashed potatoes, called "Brootsheen," with a big dot of butter in the center. Shortly afterwards I went to bed exhausted. I imagined the bed was rocking back and forth from side to side, just like I was sailing on the boat again. It felt strange to sleep in a foreign bed, in a quiet room, without my brother and sisters. Cousin Nancy slept in the other bed.

The next morning I was awakened by a rooster's loud wake-up call, and I laid still for another few minutes in the big double bed, just observing my new surroundings. This was the second bedroom, and it was furnished with two double beds, a chair, and a trunk. The walls were whitewashed and it had three windows. There was a window facing the front of the house, and as I looked out I noticed a garden, some red-currant bushes, and fields stretching out into the distance. At the back and side-bedroom windows there were black-currant bushes and two haystacks.

Gran appeared at the bedroom door and said, "Child, come and have your breakfast."

"I have to go to the toilet," I told her.

Gran led me through the kitchen and out the back door, and said, "Child, do what you have ta do over near the pigs' manure straw heap."

What a surprise—no indoor plumbing or running water! Although our home in Govan did not have a bathtub or shower, it did have an indoor toilet in the hall, a cold water faucet in the kitchen, and a black cast-iron sink.

After I did my duty, I was handed a small, white-enamel basin filled with cold water, and Gran instructed me, "Wash yur hands and face and comb yur hair."

Granda was having a big mug of tea, and he boiled an egg for my breakfast. He placed the egg in an empty can, poured water in it, and sat the can on top of red-hot turf to boil. While it boiled he instructed me, "Beatrice, kneel on my big chair and say your morning prayers." This I obediently did, while gazing up at the picture on the wall of the *The Sacred Heart Of Jesus*.

Soon my uncle Marcus arrived, along with Uncle Jimmy and Gran, who were giving Marcus a tour of the farm. We all sat down to tea and Irish bread, called "scone," and I ate my egg. As I sat eating at the kitchen table, I spotted a tall, wooden dresser to the right-hand side of the front door, filled with dishes, plates, platters, mugs, and flowered milk pitchers, all set out in a row. The dishes were white with blue painted pictures of birds and pretty flowers. Underneath was a small cupboard, and when I opened it, there was a huge block of salt. Along another wall was a wooden bench filled with pails for milking the cows, and tin cans and big, black pots with lids sat on the floor underneath the bench. On the wall above this bench were three large hooks used for hanging coats, scarves, and caps. Lower down on the wall were long nails, sometimes used to hang up a newly-caught hare or rabbit. I can remember seeing these helpless creatures hanging upside down off these nails, still breathing, with tears running down their poor faces.

Gran and Granda's big chairs sat at each side of the fireside, which had a mantelpiece with assorted items on top. I remember the fireplace had an iron, gate-like crane that could be moved in and out. There were lots of holes in the center of this crane and a piece of iron, called a crook, was inserted into these holes. It could be inserted to whatever height was needed for cooking food, boiling the clothes, or kettle, or pots.

Off the kitchen and toward the back end of the house was the entrance to the dairy. This is where they kept the brown, earthenware crocks of milk, which were churned into butter. The milk was poured into a wooden barrel that had a top with a hole in the center. A big stick with a round bottom shaped like a dinner plate, only thicker, was then inserted into the hole. The churn had to be held with both hands and moved vigorously up and down. This had to be kept on the go forever, it seemed. After many minutes of labor, Gran would come over to the barrel, lift off the lid and skim the yellow stuff off the top. She then proceeded to make little shapes of butter from the skimmings, using two wooden spatulas to accomplish this task.

Next to the dairy was a small bedroom where my uncle Jimmy slept. He was a marvelous man who used to sing songs to me when I was ill and bedridden. One song still remains engraved in my mind, though for the life of me I do not know who wrote it:

If you ever go to Ireland, will you take this message for me?
To a dear old Irish lady, sure she's sweet as an angel can be.
You'll find the white house, where the green shamrocks grow
and the mountains sweep down to the sea.
If you ever go to Ireland, would you kiss my old mother for me?

During the following weeks, while Uncle Jimmy was out working in the fields, Granda showed me around the farm. He would lead me by the hand out the back door to show me the chickens and baby chicks, the ducks, turkeys, geese, pigs, cows, two cats, and a collie dog named Rover. Then he showed me the cow shed, that he called "The Byre". This building contained two cows that peed and crapped so much, I was amazed none of it got into the milk buckets! The shed had a back door, which led into the potato, parsnip, turnip, pea, cabbage, rhubarb, onion, and carrot field.

To the right of the cow shed was the pig sty, and to the left stood the barn. The pigs smelled bad! They looked so cute, but their manure and straw, which they wallowed in, was horrible. In the barn were a horse and a donkey. I remember the donkey would hang its head over the gate and cry, "Hee-haw, hee-haw!" I felt so sorry for him because I figured he was in pain or quite hungry to be making such a ruckus.

Next to the barn was a gate that opened into the big garden, and to the left side of the garden was the chicken coop, nicknamed "The Hen House." This coop looked like a little stable perched upon three wooden legs. At dusk the chickens would automatically go into their home and go to sleep sitting up. I figured they should sleep lying down, like dogs and cats, but they didn't. I wondered, "How can they sleep like that and not fall off their roosts?"

A large, concrete tank held rainwater, which dripped off the gutters of the roof. This tank butted up against a shed named "The Boiler House." Inside stood a very large pot with a lid on it that was used for boiling potatoes, nettles, and dandelion flowers for the animals. Adjoining the shed was a room where the chicken seed was stored. I found it amusing to see the chickens running wild whenever Gran opened the door to get seed to feed them. Outside of the barn, in the barnyard, were concrete troughs filled with water for the fowl to drink out of.

My uncle Marcus only stayed for one week, as he had to return to Glasgow to his job as a welder. I was upset and lonely after he left me there with these strangers who were my granda and gran. To me, they seemed old and obviously not thrilled to have me, a sick child, imposing on them. They had already raised ten children of their own: nine sons and one daughter, plus my cousin Nancy. Two uncles, Gerry and Willy, were deceased.

The countryside seemed so quiet to me, compared to my home in Scotland. I was accustomed to hearing the tram cars clanking along the Govan Road and the men fighting and arguing outside of the bar below my bedroom window at closing time. Here in Ireland, there seemed to be an ominous stillness in the air. Even in the middle of the day the only real audible sounds were birds chirping and the chickens quietly clucking. Even the air tasted different because it was fresh and clean, especially compared to the soot we inhaled daily in Govan. Here the only pollution came from burning peat moss in the open-hearth fire-places, which was so effervescent when compared to the coal-burning smell to which I was accustomed.

I was afraid to sleep in the dark bedroom, which became pitch black after my grandparents turned off the kerosene lamps. When I was at home in Govan, the room where I slept, and the kitchen, were always lit by the street lamps which shone through the smoke-layered glass. I simply could not adjust to the inky darkness of the room. For some reason, which I believe was related to my fear of the darkness, I started wetting the bed. Sometimes I dreamt that I was sitting on the toilet, and I peed and peed. Finally Gran became very angry with me, so she made me a bed of straw on the concrete floor of her bedroom, in the corner, next to the window, and placed a cover on top of it. My new bed felt jabby when I first laid on it, but after two nights it settled down. When Gran renewed the straw, it was always jabby again. She even made up a cute poem for me about my wetting the bed: "Pissy arse, pissy arse, hide for shame. The dogs in the country know your name." I was comforted to think that so many dogs all over Ireland knew me.

I adjusted well to my new surroundings, except that certain things on the farm upset me. A chicken or any other fowl being slaughtered terrorized me. Sometimes I had to accompany my gran while she did this deed by strangling the life out of them. However, whenever a goose met its demise, I was presented with its windpipe to play with, which sounded like a goose whistle when I blew into it.

One day the king of the chickens, "Rooster Boy," met his fate. I protested, "No! No! Why pick him?" Gran said he was annoying the hens too much. After putting up a gallant fight to the very end, Rooster Boy was cleaned, washed, his feathers were plucked, and he was cooked for dinner that night. Oh, how I missed the handsome bird, with his brownish golden feathers gleaming in the sunlight, as he pranced very importantly around the farm yard. No more wake-up calls at early morning with a "cock-a-doodle-doo."

Some of my meals were different and were specially made for me. One in particular, which I might have found edible had I not seen it being made, was blood pudding. A newly-killed chicken could be seen hanging upside down, a large basin placed underneath it to catch the dripping blood. A type of corn-meal flour was then added and mixed into the bowl of blood. This amalgam was then sautéed, cooked, and fed to me. I was advised to eat it because my health was so bad, and this concoction could help to improve it. Other times I was fed a raw egg, whipped up in a cup, or egg yolk whipped with sugar, or warm buttermilk in a tin mug called a pondjer.

In front of the barnyard were turf squares all stacked into one big heap. This was used as fuel for the fire for heat and cooking. There was a gate next to this pile that led through a "Boreen," a small path, into a narrow, smaller field. I was forbidden to go in there unaccompanied, since there was a spring well in the ground, and my grandparents were fearful that I would fall into it and drown.

The old mother pig usually spent her days out in this field, which is how she got so dirty. Whenever my cousin Nancy or my grandparents called out to the pig, "Hurrish, Hurrish," she would come running and snorting up to the gate. The big, old sow then proceeded to rub her body up against the gate to scratch herself, which greatly amused me.

To keep me occupied and out of their hair, my grandparents gave me odd jobs to do. One very important task was emptying the big, white chamber pot, which they kept underneath their bed. I was terror stricken when carrying it from the bedroom, into the parlor, through the kitchen, and out the back door without spilling any of its contents. What a relief to dispose of it by tossing it on the pigs' manure heap. Then it had to be scrubbed, which was done with cold ashes from the fireplace and cold water. Finally, this urinal had to be shined and polished. The entire process was time consuming, and my grandparents were pleased with me for a job well done.

Dinner on the farm was in the evening, whereas at home in Govan we ate dinner at twelve noon. Gran and my cousin Nancy were good cooks who baked their own bread and cakes, and they allowed me to assist them whenever they baked. White flour was scarce, and I sifted it through a clean nylon stocking. I also helped to clean the eggs, which were sold or exchanged for food when the delivery truck did its rounds to the farms. Frank, the delivery man, was always a welcome visitor.

In the evenings it was fun to tramp through the fields to fetch the cows home. The cows knew when milking time was near, and I walked behind them and led them to the cow shed to be milked by Uncle Jimmy or Cousin Nancy. Everyone worked hard on the farm.

In the big garden, on the left side of the cottage, grew two red-currant bushes and a myriad of black-currant bushes, which I enjoyed picking. Gran made delicious jam out of them. Gran, Nancy and I would pick the berries off of the bushes, remove their stems, and boil them in the big, black, iron pot. We would then add lots of sugar and let them boil for a few hours. After they cooled Gran would pour the mixture into special, wax-sealed jars. This way the jam lasted for a long, long time.

When my health improved, I was sent to Killeen Duff school. To reach the school I walked barefoot in good weather, just like the other children. Since the roads were not paved, the little, sharp stones dug into my feet, but eventually I got accustomed to this. I also found a shortcut to the school by climbing over ditches and tramping through the fields. The stone-house school had two classrooms and two teachers, Master

Kelly and his wife, Mrs. Kelly. What a drastic difference between this school and St. Anthony's School at home.

We were taught the Irish language, and I quickly learned to count, say a prayer, bless myself, and answer my name in Irish. When I had to go to the toilet, I had to make this request in Irish, too. The toilets were outhouses in a field. Since there was no running water, the latrines were dry and consisted of a concrete bench with four round holes on top to sit on. They were quite cold during the Irish winter.

In the winter time, when a chicken or baby pig became sick, it was placed in a big, wooden tea chest beside the turf fireside and spoon-fed until it got better. Whenever the cows had calves, they were bottle-fed with milk, and then later given a pail of milk to drink. Nights were pleasant, and neighbors visited one another. These visitors were known as "ramblers." Gran advised me to sit silently on the stone floor beside the fireside, since "Children should be seen and not heard." Everyone remarked what a fine-looking and quiet child I was. As I sat listening to them talking, it seemed like I was being read a story. Letters from loved ones in England and far-off America were read, while the men smoked pipes. Even Gran had a small, white clay pipe. But there was no radio in the house, like the one that my parents played regularly, and I was a lonely child.

A tall, beautiful woman, with shoulder-length, black hair, lived a short distance from the Dowd home. Dressed in black and wearing a black hat, she cycled past on her way to the village of Easkey to shop or attend mass. I was told to ignore her, and so I was surprised to discover that she was really my aunt Janey. She was known as "The Widow." Apparently Janey had been of the Protestant faith, and she became a Catholic when she fell in love and married my uncle Willy Dowd. They had no children, and my uncle died of gangrene after he twisted and tore his leg on a horse-cart wheel. For some reason she was never accepted by my grandparents, and Gran became angry if I visited this woman's cottage or even spoke to her, but I did anyway.

I was allowed to visit the Connor home, Cousin Nancy's relatives. The old man who lived there was Nancy's other grandfather and the two sons were her uncles. Poor old Granda Connor usually sat in a corner of the kitchen, and his head kept shaking. Apparently he had Parkinson's disease. I was dying to ask him if the shaking ever stopped when he lay down in his bed to sleep, but I never did.

Gran grew stick-like twigs in the big garden, and whenever I misbehaved or gave her any back talk, she would whack my legs and behind with one of them. Granda, on the other hand, used those sticks to make round baskets that were wonderful for carrying turf, boiled nettles, potatoes for the animals, or laundry on wash day. I secretly wished all the sticks could be made into baskets.

The laundry was soaked in clear, crystal-like, tiny stones called "washing soda." Nancy or Gran then placed the clothing in a black, iron pot and hung it on the crook crane, over the big, blazing turf fire, to boil. After half an hour the pot was removed from the fire and allowed to cool. We then used a washboard to rub the dirty laundry up and down on until it was clean. A long rope hung in the big garden for drying, and some of our clothes were simply put on the grass or hedges to dry.

Ironing was a chore indeed. Cousin Nancy or Gran removed one of the two triangular-shaped irons that were kept red hot in the turf hearth. The one iron had to be retrieved with iron tongs, and the other iron was then inserted in its place. The hot iron was then allowed to cool for a while and then the person ironing would wrap a towel around the handle and use it to iron Granda's and Uncle Jimmy's shirts and collars. Once this iron cooled, the one that was previously inserted in the fireplace would be removed and the cold iron put in its place. The iron had an opening for inserting the triangular, hot irons. This was the way they heated them for ironing.

Granda and Uncle Jimmy were a sight to behold whenever they shaved. They used a leather belt, soap, and a razor that looked like a knife. The belt was used to sharpen the razor. When shaving, both men used a special mirror which stood on the dressing table in my grandparent's bedroom. I remember it had an adjustable wooden frame with a stand underneath.

My gran was very popular, and all the neighbors and villagers knew her. Even the police sergeant visited her home. She was a remarkable woman in many ways, and skilled in the use of old-fashioned health cures. I recall one time when I got a sty on my eye, Gran cut a thorn from a rosebush in the front garden, barely touched my eye with it, and the eye healed quickly. If I cut my foot, the cure was to simply walk in cow poop. For constipation, Gran used senna pods. These were brown leaves that had to be soaked in water overnight. Then they were strained and made into senna tea that tasted dreadful! I tried to refuse drinking this horrible concoction, but while Gran and Granda held me, Uncle Jimmy poured the tea into my mouth. Half of the tea spilled all over me!

One day the mailman delivered a package. Curious, I waited to see what was in it, but Gran did not open it. Sometime later I was looking underneath her bed to retrieve the chamber pot, and I came across the package. I opened it and discovered that the package had been sent by my mom in Scotland and its contents were for me. Inside were new school clothes, a skirt and blouse, a sweater, a pair of brown leather shoes, and white socks. Since my cousin Nancy was out riding her new bicycle and Uncle Jimmy and my grandparents were doing yard work, I tried all these items on. Everything fit me except the shoes, which were too small and tight. However, I neglected to inform Gran that I had been snooping under her bed, and when she found out, she was infuriated and beat the hell out of me with a stick.

On Sundays we attended church in the village of Easkey, two miles from the cottage, and "a good walk for the legs," as the neighbors often remarked. Gran dressed me up in my new clothes, but when I told her, "The new shoes are too tight and hurt my feet," she did not believe me. The only way I could manage to walk was by curling my toes in tight, which was so painful that I felt like crying, but I knew that Gran would only whack me for complaining. I remember that Roslea Road was a long, long road that Sunday. My heals blistered and became infected.

A family named Carnegie usually met us as we were walking to attend church. Two of their daughters often walked with me to school. They were not Catholic, and the church they attended was Protestant and stood to the left side of the village, while the Catholic church was further along to the right. The village was quaint with a few small shops, two in particular were called "Brogans" and "Rafters." I also recall that on the left side of the road, going toward the village, was a cemetery with big, stone crosses, and we blessed ourselves every time we passed it. The Carnegies owned a pony and buggy and often gave us a ride to church if they were going by as we walked to Easkey.

Three other uncles and an aunt lived a few miles away from Roslea Road, where my grandparents cottage stood. Uncle Dominic and his wife, Francis, lived in Tubbercurry. Uncle Frank lived in Callaghanally in Clooney while Uncle Danny lived in Dunmoran Strand in Screen. As a matter of fact, he was the mailman in Screen. My grandparents' only daughter, my aunt Sara, lived in Culeens with her husband Sean Lynagh.

Whenever Uncle Danny visited Gran he fascinated me. The first thing he did upon his arrival was to remove his fake, glass eye, put it in an old cup of cold water and place the cup on the dresser. I would peek into the cup and the blue eye would stare back at me. For the life of me, I could not understand how he could take his eye out and put it back again! My grandparents found this whole ordeal very amusing.

Auction Day, which was also called Fair Day, was an exciting event for everyone except me. I absolutely hated to see any of my animal friends being transported away by uncle Jimmy, especially my pigs. I often overheard Granda say they would make "great eating." Granda would sit by the turf fireside during Fair Day to await Jimmy's arrival.

Gran would cry if uncle Jimmy was late coming home on Fair Day, worried that he should lose the money he received from selling the animals. But he usually arrived home by 11 PM, a little tipsy, and presented her with the cash. On one occasion I overheard, "Ten pounds," which was considered a good price for selling an animal.

One day we had two welcomed visitors from Glasgow, my aunt Annie, who was Cousin Nancy's mother, and Cousin Chrissy, who was Nancy's teenage sister. Chrissy was a pretty, blue-eyed, bubbly, blonde girl. Although Nancy loved Annie dearly, she called our grandparents "Ma" and "Da." Her mom and sister stayed for only a week's vacation.

Another time a pretty lady visited from England, and stayed for tea and cakes. She had been a neighbor who left Ireland to find employment in England. My grandparents could not get over her appearance because she wore lots of make-up. I recall she wore rouge, painted nails, leg tan, and dyed hair, which Gran called "paint and powder." They considered her ruined, and England was to blame. Both my grandparents said, "God help any girl who marries an Englishman because they are doomed for certain and will have no luck."

I loved the visitors but I believe they also brought unwelcome visitors with them—lice. My long hair, which was never washed, was a perfect place for them to flourish. I did not know they were dirty or they were called "lousy." I just ran my fingers through my hair and picked them out rather easily. I would line them up on the window sills of the bedroom and marvel at their yellow, waxy bodies with black dots in the center. They were fun to play with. They made a crackling noise when I squished them with my thumbnail.

Uncle Jimmy sprayed the potato crop with a chemical called "Bluestone," which was stored in big barrels in the barn. After spraying he told me I could not play in the potato field or pick potatoes, because the Bluestone was to keep them from going bad or rotting. I guess the stuff was pretty poisonous, but I didn't know any better. Luckily I always listened to Granda, so I did not go into the field.

Everyday at noon time far-off church bells would chime. My grandparents told me that this ringing of the bells was called "The Angelous." I knew not to speak at this special time. Men would remove their caps or hats, kneel on the ground, and then bless themselves with the sign of the cross. Irish farmers believed, and still do believe, that God was always involved in the health of their crops.

On my many adventures I realized how lovely the farm and its surroundings were to me. The fields were so green, and it was fun wandering through them. Within walking distance from my grandparents home, I made many friends, but they were all older people. There were no young friends to play with except at school, and no young children ever visited us, so I was often rather lonely.

To the left of our cottage stood a stone, gray-colored cottage, the home of the Flannery's, Patrick and Winifred, who were nicknamed "Pat" and "Winny." They were brother and sister, and neither of them were married. They had a sister who was a nun. Their farm was fairly large, and although they were always busy working, they never were too busy to talk to me. They said, "You are a grand girl." They also loved to listen to my Scottish accent as it was so different from the Irish.

A narrow road to the left side of the Flannery home led to a tree-lined river that had lots of stones in the water and a bridge to walk across to the other side. It was so still and peaceful, and I would sit for long periods of time gazing into the sparkling-clear river, watching the tree shadows dancing across it. I never met anyone there, no matter how often I went. But for some reason, whenever I walked over the small bridge and reached the other side of the river, I became afraid. The pathway was very narrow, and the trees, with their overhanging branches blocking the sunlight, made this place rather ominous. I never stayed to see what was on the other side of the river. Maybe the "walking anti-Christ." Whenever Gran was really upset with me, she called me this name. She would yell, "I declare to God, Beaty, you are a walking anti-Christ!" Since this anti-Christ enjoyed walking like I did, I was always on the lookout for it, curious to see what it looked like, but scared nonetheless.

Although Gran was very moody, on her happy days she would call me "agraw" or "astore," which were loving endearments in Irish. I always enjoyed these moods because she would sit me on her knee and tell me folklore stories. I recollect one night she told me the story of "The Banshee." In Ireland, the Banshee is the fairy elf, a not-very-good-looking woman with long, yellow hair. When a person is near death, the Banshee comes around in the night and stands near the window of his or her home, crying, wailing, and combing her hair. As I recited my prayers before returning to my straw bed that night, I said an extra prayer, "Please God, don't let anyone in this cottage die."

My granda taught me a child's prayer: "Here I lay me down to sleep, I give the Lord my soul to keep. Four corners on my bed. Four angels on my spread. Matthew, Mark, Luke, and John. God bless this bed that I lay on. If any evil spirit comes to trouble me, Lord Jesus, save me. Amen." I would then lay awake in bed, petrified in the dark bedroom, while my grandparents slept comfortably in their big double bed.

The parlor was seldom used, since it was the special room in the house for entertaining visitors. Gran loved her parlor and it was obvious to see why. The room was lavishly furnished and had a carpet like an Oriental rug. A polished dining-room table and four chairs stood in the middle of room, and against the walls two sideboards displayed china dishes and silverware. There was also a white, mantled fireplace, like the one my grandparents had in their bedroom, and two tall lamps with flowered shades.

I must have related to my grandparents the sexual molestation incident by the neighbor boy that I had experienced in Scotland two years earlier, because one day they informed me that I would be going for a nice bus ride. The dear souls walked me to the village where we boarded a bus to Ballinna, which is in Co Mayo. A doctor visit followed, and he examined me. My grandparents bought me a bag of hard candy and a drink of mineral water, and I even had my picture taken. I really enjoyed the bus ride and all the attention. When we arrived home to the cottage, there was a pleasant surprise waiting for me—a cute black and white puppy dog, which Uncle Jimmy named Wavy. Wavy followed me everywhere, and we became close friends.

Traveling people, whom my grandparents called "tinkers," often stopped by the cottage. They made tin cans and mugs. One day a lady tinker came to the door and asked Gran for some tea and sugar. When she gave her these two items, the tinker said, "God bless you, ma'am," and continued begging for other things—a dropeen of milk or an egg. Gran invited her into her home and fed her tea and bread. I heard Gran tell Granda that the tinker lady was with child, but I did not see any child accompanying her.

My dad visited in the winter, but he stayed only a few days. I seldom saw him, as he was visiting with old friends and drinking at The Seafield Hotel, the only hotel in the vicinity. The building was pale yellow and looked like a palace to my young eyes. The Kenneys, who were two very polite, older, spinster sisters, owned it. They drove a big, black car, and when they delivered my half-shot dad back to the cottage, they remarked that I was the spitting image of him, with my blue eyes and curly, wavy hair. I had completely forgotten that I had a family, and my dad was only a visitor to me.

Poor Dad was the black sheep of this large, Irish family. He was employed as a vet's assistant in Ireland, and he and the vet were drinking buddies. Dad's girlfriend was a neighbor girl, and he got her pregnant, which was considered a disgrace to both families. Their baby girl was kept a big secret. Dad really loved his girlfriend and never got over her. I do not recall the reason why they never got married, but I often heard that Granda gave him an awful beating and forced him to leave Ireland quickly.

One day, not too long after Dad visited, my mom arrived, along with my brother Ed, sister Rose, and the baby, Patricia, to enjoy a two weeks holiday. My mom was absolutely appalled at my dirty appearance, especially my hair that was never shampooed or washed for the year I lived in Ireland. She stood me on a chair to bathe me, and she had to scrub the dirt out of my groin and private parts. She yelled at Gran, saying it was a disgrace to leave a poor child in such a filthy condition. However, Mom was grateful to my grandparents for saving my life. These two old people had done their best in caring for a child they could not be bothered with. It was really too much to have expected of them and unfair all the way around.

Chapter 3

Home Again

I do not remember the return trip to my home in Scotland, but the excitement of getting to know my family again was overwhelming to me. When I arrived in Glasgow, I was treated like a celebrity. All the neighbors welcomed me with open arms, and they remarked on my healthy-looking appearance, chubby body, and acquired Irish accent. I talked nonstop and sang the songs that my dear uncle Jimmy had taught to me. Even the shopkeepers requested me to sing songs for them, and I felt very important, indeed.

Alas, the fun times stopped, and it was time for me to return to school at St. Anthony's. Unfortunately, everything I had been taught before I became ill was all but forgotten. I was considered a dunce because while in Ireland I learned in the Irish language. I could count to twenty in Irish, but did not know my ABCs or numbers in English.

Although I was placed in class with other eight year olds, my education was at a five-year-old's level. My teacher was either too busy to notice me or assumed I was plain stupid. I was considered very Irish, which my parents found amusing, but at this age I did not pay any attention.

Shortly afterwards the time approached for my school friends and me to make our First Holy Communion. The anticipation and excitement of the big day was almost unbearable. My parents purchased a pretty, white, long-sleeved, satin dress for me, and I also received a short, white veil and white shoes. After I spent a painful night sleeping on the big knots of rag curlers, Mom styled my hair in ringlet curls. All the boys and girls looked elegant, wearing their best attire.

Sadly, a few weeks earlier, one of the girls in my class at school had died suddenly. Ann was a delicate, pretty girl with brown eyes and long, straight, blond hair. She suffered from a heart condition, and was buried wearing her communion dress. Her death upset me dreadfully. I cried and asked Mom, "Ma, why did Ann have to die?"

"Your friend is now an angel up in heaven, Beatrice," Mom responded.

I thought, "How wonderful to have a friend who is an angel in heaven," and I did not feel so sad anymore. Then I wondered, "Could I get a step ladder long enough to climb up to the sky where heaven is and visit my friend?"

Mom was kept busy at home, since there were now four of us children to care for, as well as Dad. We also had acquired a boarder by this time to help alleviate some of the strain caused by too much rent and too little money. Old Joe Whitaker was Irish and from Dublin. He was employed part time at Fairfield shipyard. He had learned to knit while in the service, and knit socks and even a lavender-colored dress for my sister Patricia. Although my dad called him "an old woman," we all loved him.

Fairfield Working Men's Club

Being home again with my family was wonderful, although it was difficult for me to adjust to it at first. The constant noise of tram cars rattling and clanging around the corner on Govan Road kept me awake at night. On Friday and Saturday nights, there were always noisy men cursing outside the bar at closing time. The bars opened at 11:30 AM and stayed open until 2:30 PM. Then they opened again at 5 PM and stayed open until 9 PM or so. All this commotion going on right below our bedroom window was quite distracting. The police would arrive in "The Black Maria" van and escort men away for being drunk and disorderly. Especially on the weekends it could be close to 11 PM before it was peaceful enough for me to sleep! What an awful change compared to the peaceful, rural spot in Ireland.

Dad was no longer employed at the shipyard, but worked at Harlands Foundry, a company that made boilers and parts for ships. It was nicknamed the "Glass House" because it looked like a plant green house with dull, white glass. Dad told me he did back-breaking jobs where the heat was unbearable, and would outstretch his hands to show me his calluses. I felt sad that poor Dad killed himself working to lift large bags of coke to keep the furnaces going.

Although Dad drank heavily every weekend, he was a good, dependable, hard worker. He was instrumental in getting employment for people, usually Irish men. These Irishmen arrived at our door, often with a worn, leather, brown suitcase and only hope in their pockets. They had sailed to the Glasgow-Broomilaw dock from Ireland in search of work. My parents did their utmost to accommodate them temporarily in our already over-crowded home or would arrange accommodations for them with their friends. These men remained forever grateful to my parents.

Every Saturday afternoon most of the children in our neighborhood attended the matinee at The Vogue, one of the local cinemas. The place would be packed with noisy children. Before the show started, Uncle Harry, a funny and wonderful elderly man, entertained us. We loved him. He told funny stories and had us sing along to songs which we all knew—mostly war time songs and others heard on the radio at home. His good-bye signature song was "Pack Up Your Troubles," and he would wave his snow white handkerchief at us. The children went wild, and we would yell, "Cheerio, Uncle Harry, until this time next week!" Then we would throw our hats and sweaters up into the air. One time I foolishly tossed my new coat up, and it never came back.

Shortly afterwards, the big, satin curtains covering the screen opened and the show began. What a bargain for a sixpenny bit! We saw cartoons, cowboys, and movies. We cheered the good guys and booed and stamped our feet loudly at the bad guys. The show was different each week, with some being continuous shows, so we were anxious to attend the following week to see the rest of the story.

When I arrived home after losing my new coat, my parents were not pleased with me—imagine losing a new coat. They scolded, "What a careless and heedless thing to do! You should have known better and shown a good example since you are the eldest child."

A favorite game was skipping rope, which was enjoyable, and according to Mom, "Good exercise." One day while I was skipping along the street, minding my own business, I happened to pass by a neighbor girl who had broken her leg. She was walking with the aid of a walking cane and talking to her friend. Her friend borrowed the cane, and for some ungodly reason, grabbed me around the neck with it as I skipped past. I promptly fell on my face, and the impact of the concrete broke my two front teeth and smashed my lips. You should have seen the blood—what a mess and state I was in!

I ran over to a neighbor lady who often sat on the window ledge beside our home. But instead of assisting me, she gently pushed me away, and so I ran upstairs to my mom. Mom told me to get a tomato off of our sideboard and suck on it to stop the bleeding. She said the acid in the tomato would help heal my mouth.

Instead, my gums became infected with boils, and Mom had to escort me to the dental hospital once a month. The doctor at the hospital tried to save my two front teeth, as only half of them were broken off, and he hoped to crown or cap them. Alas, the teeth eventually had to be extracted, and Mr. Boston, the family dentist, did this labor. He was very kind and gave me Novocain and three pennies for being such a brave girl. He then sent me home to Mom with a piece of gauze stuck in my mouth.

Mr. Boston made a cute little denture plate with two front teeth on it for me. My parents were pleased because it helped my gummy appearance, and I was inclined to smile more often after I received my new teeth. Brother Ed and Sister Rose were amazed when I removed them and put them back in my mouth. At first I was a big attraction at school and in the neighborhood until I got called "gumsy" or "doodles" by the other children, and I became very self-conscious about my teeth after that.

My little sister Patricia was three around this time, and she was a pretty, cute little thing. However, she had a heart murmur, and so my parents worried about her and gave her a little more attention than the rest of us. Little Patricia realized this and was especially clingy to Ma. At times Ed and I would slap her and call her a whiner. Then if she cried, we would powder her eyelids and beg her not to tell our parents. Sometimes she told and we got scolded and she got cuddled. However, we children loved each other and were all very close. We had to stick together and stand on our own two feet in good times and bad.

Dad was working hard at the foundry during the week and then drinking heavily on weekends. He became moody and argued with Mom. Sometimes he would get loud and nasty and sing Irish songs out the open kitchen window just to annoy the neighbors. He would tell me, "Your mother and I are going to separate." Then he would ask, "Who do you love most, your ma or me?"

I replied, "I love both of you!" I cried and wanted to go to sleep but was kept awake instead by their relentless fighting.

One Saturday morning I entered the kitchen, which was where my parents slept. My poor mom was crying softly in bed. Her face was a mess, and her left eye was so purple and black and swollen that she appeared distorted, which scared me. Dad was asleep beside her.

When I asked her, "What happened to your eye, Ma?" she lied.

"I tripped and fell into the corner of the kitchen table." She was seven months pregnant at this time. I believed her, but I was very sad because she looked so grotesque that I was afraid of her.

Two months later Aunt Lily arrived at our home to assist us, while the local midwife helped Mom deliver a beautiful, ten-pound, curly-haired baby girl, a new sister for us. The nurse midwife was called "The Green Lady" because she usually wore a dark green coat and hat. She looked stern but kindly. She visited Mom for five days, which was the usual procedure whenever a baby was born at home.

Rose, age 5

I overheard The Green Lady asking my mom, "Mrs. Dowd, why didn't you press charges against your husband?" Then she said, "There is no way you can convince me that you got that awful black eye by falling against a table." The eye injury was to bother my dear mom for the rest of her life. Although she never went to the eye doctor to alleviate her pain, it watered and itched and she rubbed it constantly.

When Mom looked better, about a month later, it was time to christen the baby. Relatives and friends arrived at the church, and the air was filled with joy. My youngest sister was named Violet Lillian—Lillian after Mom's sister. We all enjoyed the party. Afterwards it was customary to present new babies with cash gifts.

I recall a neighbor boy sitting on the stairs outside our door, waiting patiently for us to present him with the customary two cookies stuck together with margarine, and two silver half-crown coins placed inside. If the baby had been a boy, the gift would be presented to the first girl we met outside of our own family, usually a neighbor's child. The boy who received the cookie gift this time was the brother of the young man who sexually molested me. I did not understand that the boy had saved me—he was always pleasant and never discussed anything of the incident with me.

Baby Violet was an adorable and good-natured baby. She resembled my sister Rose, as both of them had curly hair. However, Violet had dark brown eyes, whereas Rose's were green. Since Ma breast-fed Violet, she received large cans of dried milk, orange juice, and cod-liver oil, which we went and got from the local clinic, as did everyone else. I must admit some of us were a little envious of the new arrival, but not my brother Ed. He loved his baby sister right from the start and would lovingly pick the tiny pieces of cotton wool from between her tiny toes. This probably came off the cotton balls that Ma used to bathe her.

One time Mom sent me to visit the O'Briens, old friends of the family who were rapidly becoming feeble. The O'Briens were from Ireland. Mr. O'Brien wore a black suit and always had a cap on his head. Mrs. O'Brien was fat and wore a knitted, dark navy blue shawl. Her silver hair was pinned back into a roll at the back of her head. She was a talkative lady, with blue eyes, and a round, friendly, happy face.

Mom sent me with a pot full of her delicious "Scotch Broth," which she cooked every Saturday night. Mom was very kind in this respect, and she often said, "One never misses what they can spare, and God will reward us for being kind to these poor old souls who live across the landing from us."

Another day while I was visiting the couple, Mrs. O'Brien had wet her panties. She was sitting on a chair beside the fireplace, her panties down at her ankles. She asked me, "Well, lassie, can you help me remove these and get them in a basin of cold water to soak them?" The dear lady was so grateful that she insisted on giving me three pennies, even though I resisted and said I was not allowed to accept anything.

When I got home, my mom was livid with anger at me for accepting the money. She gave me a good slap for disobeying her orders. When my dad arrived home from work three hours later, Mom related the story to him. He removed his black leather belt, grabbed me by the arm, and whacked me on the back, legs, and behind. The belt which he used on me had been a gift to him from my uncle Marcus, who had purchased it in Germany. It had a buckle on each end, and I often wished it had stayed in Germany.

Although we did not have a bathtub in our home, all of us were very clean people. We simply boiled a big kettle full of water and poured it into the basins and pails reserved for bathing or doing laundry. One person at a time went into the bedroom to wash in private. I'd cover myself with a towel and call my sister to wash my back. Next I went to the tiny toilet to wash private parts, then I'd take the basin into the bedroom or kitchen and soak my feet. Last, I'd wash out the basin for the next person, fill it with water, and put it on to heat. Later on I'd go and wash my sister's back when called. We always wore our underwear to bed, as children were taught to be modest and not expose body parts.

Mom did not believe in potty chairs for toilet training children. She said it should be done one time and in the proper way. Hence, it was not unusual to pass by our small toilet at the end of the hall and witness poor Violet sitting on the throne while hanging on for dear life to the back of a kitchen chair. I guess it was pee or swim! During those years, we did not have toilet tissue. We used cut-up newspapers to wipe our bottoms.

Dad really enjoyed reading newspapers, and on Sundays we got two newspapers. He would read and reread them as he mumbled to himself. Sometimes, if any of us had the trots, at least half of poor Dad's newspapers would be flushed down the toilet by the time he arrived home from work.

When my sister Violet was two years old, she was considered a "big girl now" and got to sleep with Rose, Patricia, and me in our big double bed. My brother Ed had his own bed, and since we only had one bedroom in our home, he slept in a recessed bed set in an alcove in the wall that had curtains for privacy.

We children had our own special friends to play with, but since they were not allowed into our home, we had to play outside with them. My parents feared they might drink the milk or eat our bread. The games which we played were: kick the can, tag, and playball. A very popular item at this time was "Peery," and most little girls owned one. A Peery was a small, wooden spinning top with a tiny stick-like whip to hit it with. We colored the top in circles with crayons, so it resembled a beautiful rainbow as it bounced off the ground, and kept us occupied for hours.

When I was eleven, my mom's friend, Lizzy Maxwell, was employed part-time cleaning offices and restrooms at the Fairfield shipyard or on the ships themselves. Since word of mouth was a good reference, she got Mom a part-time job doing the same. The company did not even provide a mop, and Mom had to work on her hands and knees. The jelly soft soap that was used for cleaning was tough on the skin, and there were no rubber gloves provided. My indignant mom's hands would bleed and crack from this torturous labor.

Her working hours revolved around our home life. She started at 6 AM and worked until 8 AM, and then returned home in time to get our

Saint Anthony's Church.

breakfast, which was a roll and margarine or oatmeal and a cup of tea. She saw us off to school, which started at 9 AM. Then Mom did her house chores, made our twelve noon dinner, sometimes rested up a bit, and then fed us supper at 5 PM. At 6 PM she returned to her job and worked until 8 PM. To top all this off, her female supervisor at the shipyard was very strict, even mean at times, with all the employees under her.

Saint Anthony's was both a primary and secondary school within walking distance of our home. The majority of the students who attended this institution of knowledge walked to school with groups of other kids. Any child walked to school by a mom was considered a spoiled brat or sissy. The school consisted mostly of female teachers, save for the headmaster, Mr. Bell. There were approximately thirty children in each classroom, and we sat two together at small, wooden desks with tiny ink wells and long-ribbed pens. Since I found the pens difficult to use, I scribbled in a scrawly writing.

We were taught the usual subjects: math, English, geography, Bible history, and religion. The city of Glasgow supplied the school with half pints of milk for every school child, and at 10 AM we got our milk break. I frequently had a roll and margarine uneaten at breakfast, and I usually consumed that quite rapidly, one gob at a time, before break time.

Our teachers were kindly, although strict at times. When a child talked in class or was rude and misbehaving she received the "tause" a thick leather belt, as punishment. We had to hold out our crossed, outstretched hands and feel the burn of the leather into our palms. If we drew away, we got another whack. Our hands seemed numb for ages afterwards.

At recess we played in the school yard, which was packed with children. There were outside toilets and they flushed. From noon until 1 PM, we got one hour for dinner, and then finished school at 4 PM.

My mom's part-time job meant extra responsibilities for me, especially during the long summer evenings, when it did not get dark until almost 11 PM. We usually helped by running errands, emptying trash, and handwashing any dirty laundry, and then we played with our friends, did our homework, and ate supper. Being the eldest child, I had to keep an eye on my three sisters, brother Ed, and my father, and I resented this very much. Dad usually arrived home from work at 7 PM, and the supper for him was always the monotonous same: a soft-boiled egg, bread and butter, and a pot of tea. I absolutely dreaded boiling the egg, which was supposed to be a three-minute egg.

Since our stove was right next to the kitchen window, the results were not always the same. My friends were noisy when playing, and I could see them below in the street from the window. I would watch enviously as they played "Heights"—jumping over a long rope held by two people, and adjusted higher, until someone won. Needless to say, I would become engrossed in the game and forget about the stinking egg!

Dad would come home, wash up, sit down at the table, and murmur to himself as he read the evening newspaper. I would serve him his supper and nervously ask, "How is your egg, Da?"

"Oh fine, pet," he'd reply.

"And the tea, how is it Da?"

"Fine. Just grand, pet."

But then when he cracked the top off the egg, I could see it was either runny and watery or hard as a stone! Later that night, after Mom arrived home from work, I could overhear him saying, "That one ruined my supper again! The tea was like dishwater and my egg was hard boiled."

Mom encouraged me to do better. She'd say, "Now, Beatrice, try to remember to look at the clock on the mantle shelf over the fireplace."

I'd say, "I'll try and time it, Ma." Then I asked, "Ma, why can't we have powdered eggs to scramble, the kind we used after the war?" Anything to make my life a little easier!

I only had to get supper on Monday through Thursday, and on Friday's we ate take-out fish and chips, tea, bread, and butter. It was wonderful not to have to get my da's supper. If the weather was nice, Mom would tell me to bathe my little sister Violet and be certain that she and the other children were presentable. We then went to meet her at the side door of the shipyard offices, and she gave us money to buy ice cream cones because she got paid on Fridays. We were so happy to see her, even if it was for less than five minutes.

During the holiday season, between Christmas and New Years, Dad escorted us to the circus and carnival, which was an annual event. We marveled at the trapeze artists as they swung from the ropes and swings and walked the tightrope without falling off. The elephants, horses, lions, tigers, and crazy monkeys and clowns were delightful. We tried our luck at the many booths. We spent time riding on the "Waltzer," the carrousel, and toy cars. Dad also got us lemonade, candy floss, and toffee apples.

One year Dad left us there by ourselves while he went to the bar. We wandered around, and somehow we lost track of where to meet him, so we just went home without him. Mom was livid and did not allow him to take us anymore.

One day Mom complained to Dad, "Eddy, I heard a scratching noise during the night, and it sounded like it came from the kitchen cupboard below the sink where we keep the wash cloths and basins." Dad thought she imagined it because Mom was deaf in her left ear due to a botched mastoid operation when she was a little girl. She said the noise was getting louder as the week progressed. To please her, he set a trap to catch whatever should appear.

We were not afraid of mice in our humble home. At night, after we all retired to bed, we could hear their little feet chasing each other around our home. In the morning, if Mom had forgotten to clean off the frying pan, we often saw tiny footprints engraved in the lard. Mom then had to clean the pan by scouring it and boiling it in water on top of the stove. They were truly amazing little creatures, climbing on top of our stove while we were sleeping.

After many nights with the trap set, a piercing scream awakened my parents, and we found a huge rat caught in the trap. Dad remarked, "It really worked hard, digging its way up from the bar beneath us to freedom in our flat." The next day, when we came home from school at noon for dinner, there was the rat that Dad had placed in an empty milk can. I was amazed at the sight of it, with its eyes wide open and its long tail hanging out over the can.

Mom suggested we dispose of it, and I got the job. She told me to take it to the rent office where we paid the monthly fee of renting our one bedroom and kitchen flat. As I entered the office there were a few customers waiting in line, so I politely said, "Excuse me," as I passed them by. I had to stand on tiptoe to reach the counter to place the container on it. When the secretary saw the rat, she screamed, and then the other office staff screamed and almost ran each other over. Mr. Black, the boss, came out of his office and reprimanded me for being a "rotten, rotten girl." However I stood my ground and said, "My mom sent this rat to you to show you what she pays her rent to get."

Mr. Black told me, "Take it to the Public Health Department further along the road."

The man at the health department was not overly concerned. He inquired as to my name and address, and I figured he must have been used to seeing or receiving dead rats. Mom laughed so heartily when I related the story of the disposal of the rat, that it was worth the effort. I scrubbed my hands and hurried back to school by 1 PM.

Every Sunday the Presbyterian church at the end of our street had a wonderful bell that chimed for half an hour between 10:30 and 11 AM. All of us except Mom attended mass. Dad was usually trying to sober himself up and attended late service at Anthony's by himself. It was amazing how he could always look so well groomed—shoes polished, wavy hair combed so perfectly, tie straight—and be half shot. He did this out of respect for God's house, the church. Dad believed that the Catholic religion was the one and only true faith because, as he often told me, "Our Lord God said to Saint Peter: "Thou art Peter and upon this Rock I will build my church, and the gates of Hell shall not prevail against it. And I will give to you the keys of the Kingdom of Heaven.'"

I often remarked to Mom that I always saw a lady friend of hers at church, and even on school days, I would spot the same woman leaving the church. The woman was a saintly Irish person who always wore big, wide-brimmed hats. Ma thought a lot of Catholics were, in general, hypocrites, and scoffed and said sarcastically, "She must have murdered someone." Ma only attended occasionally, perhaps it was because she was denied by the priest to be married in front of the altar since she was pregnant and "in a sinful state."

In the early years, attending mass was an awful ordeal for me. We were instructed not to whisper to each other, and never turn our heads to gaze around or look up to the gallery, where the choir was singing hymns. We were told that our heads might stay in a turned-around position forever. My parents also told us to never whistle anytime as this offended The Blessed Lady, God's mother, and caused her to cry in Heaven.

One of our priests, Father Reilly, always gave loud sermons denouncing those afflicted by the curse of drinking alcohol. He would hang over the pulpit, waving his arms, protesting about people who were not attending mass as they should, and always grumbling that not enough money was being given to the collection plate. When the collection plate came around, I did not put the penny in that my dad gave me, instead I kept my penny and bought a piece of chewing or bubble gum on the way home.

I also lit candles in church. There was an honesty box, but I did not have any money. I felt that it was not too dishonest to be poor. If I traveled on the tram cars and the conductor forgot to request my fare, I would be delighted. There was a box at the exit of the tram cars for forgotten fares, which I also ignored. However, our family was honest in most ways. My parents often remarked that they could leave any amount of money laying about, even a penny, and it was never touched by any of us.

Missionary priests visited St. Anthony's Church in October. It was a pleasure to listen to them relate their travel stories to us as they enlightened us about the countries and people they visited while making their rounds. Most of these missionaries performed their services in Africa, and so we collected pennies at school and in church for the "poor black babies." We also prayed for the release of Cardinal Minzenty, who was held prisoner in a foreign country for many years.

October devotions were especially enjoyable. The Latin hymns were lovely, while the smell of incense burning made me sneeze. On one occasion my mom paid a visit to the priest's house to have a talk with Father Reilly about Dad's heavy weekend drinking and verbal abuse. He did not understand her complaints, and said, "I have met Eddy many times. He is a hard-working Irishman and a fine man indeed." My mom retorted, "Huh, huh . . . why don't you pay us a visit any Friday or Saturday night and see for yourself? The key is always in the door."

A few weeks passed, and we had forgotten about Mom's remark to the priest. Dad was being his usual nasty, drunken self, pushing us all around and swearing out loud, when who should appear on the scene but Father Reilly. He just turned the key in the door and walked into our home, like Mom had suggested. Well, my dad was in a rage, and the priest became annoyed, too. Father Reilly said to Dad, "Come on, lad, go ahead and hit me!"

My da replied, "I can't hit you. You are a priest."

Father Reilly quickly tore off his white collar and said, "Forget I'm a priest. Hit me! And if you do, I'll knock the paint off your baseboards with your head!"

Even though Dad was drunk, he said, "I cannot hit a priest." We all ended up kneeling on the cold, linoleum kitchen floor saying the Rosary. Ah, Dad had met his match at last, and I thought it was hysterically amusing. We were all saddened when sometime later this good priest was sent back to Ireland, silenced, I heard. "How awful he can never speak again," we children remarked.

Occasionally on Sunday evenings we had company, usually two couples who were friends of my parents. They were Annie and Hugh Gaffney and Mary and Larry McNally who had come to play cards. Before they arrived, we were instructed not to chase each other around our flat. But once we became bored, all our good intentions were forgotten, and we would pinch or kick each other, play hide-and-seek, and crawl underneath our parents' bed. We pushed up the dust ruffle of the bed, which exposed all of our shoes and numerous other items that Mom had stashed away. We children felt guilty but only for a short while.

The Gaffneys were Irish and had two sons, Austen and Cyril, whom we seldom saw, except at school. The McNally's were very close friends of my parents, and they had been married around the same time. We called them Aunt Mary and Uncle Larry. They had a daughter,

Margaret, and two sons, Peter and Lawrence. The children visited us sometimes, and we also visited them at their home. Aunt Mary had a wonderful soprano voice, and it was a pleasure to listen to her singing.

When it was time for us to retire to our beds for the night, Mom gave us a treat of a small cake each, from a big, double plate filled with assorted cakes for the guests. We politely said, "Good night," and then quietly crept back to peep through the partly-opened kitchen door.

"Which one do you like?" we asked one another, as each of us picked one out in the hope it would not be eaten. As a guest's hand reached out to take a cake, we would say to each other, "Oh, well, there goes your cake," until eventually they were all eaten.

The next day at school I told my school friends about the delicious cakes. "You can buy a bag full of broken cakes at the bakery shop around the corner, dead cheap," they informed me. On the following Friday when I got my pocket money, I bought a bag full of assorted broken cakes and ran home to share them with my sisters and brother Ed. They tasted wonderful, and we greedily ate them up. We were completely oblivious to how we must have looked with our hands and faces covered with cream, jam, and chocolate.

Our dear sitter, Irene Spence, became ill one day. Although she no longer had to mind us, we still saw her frequently. Irene had a bad heart condition, and it was very sad for all of us when she died at the tender age of sixteen. Her parents were devastated, as were the neighbors and the local boy who lived across the street and really liked her a lot. My parents insisted that we pay our respects to Irene.

I was reluctant as we climbed the stairs to the Spence home. They graciously welcomed us and led us into the bedroom. Our beloved Irene lay in her coffin wearing a long, white dress. Her long hair hung loosely on her shoulders, and there was cotton in her nostrils. Her feet were bare. She looked so pale. I wanted her to wake up! My parents led us all away crying.

The neighbors who lived directly across from us were the Feeneys, Bill, Ella and their son, William. William was a nice little boy, about six years old, with light blond hair. Ella was a pleasant, pretty woman, and she ran the shop close to where we lived. Bill was a tall, handsome man. They also had a sick baby who cried constantly, which depressed all of us, especially my mom. Eventually the baby died, and we all watched out our kitchen window as Bill Feeney carried the tiny, white coffin to a waiting car for transport to the cemetery for burial. My mom explained to us, "It is really a blessing that God took this baby to Heaven where it will have no more pain."

Mrs. Trigenza was a widow neighbor who also lived on our landing. We called her Trigs. She was an older woman, and four of her granddaughters lived in our building. The Duncans also dwelled on our landing, and the family lived on the third floor.

Trigs was a hard worker, who, according to Mom, was "up at dawn." For two shillings a week, she washed the cement stairs plus the entrance to the flats using disinfectant and soap. Each one of the fifteen families who lived in our building were required to scrub their stair entrance way and another set of steps, called "The Dunny," that led out to the back of the building. Since the bar patrons sometimes urinated there, it required lots of disinfectant.

One of Trigs granddaughters, Ann Duncan, was my age and an only child. She was pretty, with red hair, and I was so envious of this dear, neighbor girl. Ann attended tap dance classes and wore pretty dresses and red dance shoes with bows. We often encouraged her to give us a demonstration of the latest dance steps or begged her for a ride on her new bicycle or roller skates. We did not have any of these luxuries in our home. When Ann had a birthday party, I was invited. We played musical chairs and sang childish songs, but the cake was the main attraction. The Duncans were nice and kept to themselves, as did most of our neighbors. We did not get overly involved either.

When I was nearly eleven-and-a-half, my poor dad had an accident at work. A large bag of coke fell on top of his head, fracturing his skull, and he was rushed by emergency vehicle to a special hospital and placed in the head and trauma unit. This was a shock to his two brothers, Martin and John, as they were very close to each other. My uncle Martin resembled Dad a lot, but whenever they got together and started drinking, they argued. Then Dad would refuse to talk to Uncle Martin for months on end.

When Dad returned home six weeks later, he suffered headaches and became very, very moody. With the five of us around in the evenings while Mom was out working, it did not help his discomfort having to listen to a lively bunch of children arguing, teasing, and chasing each other around the kitchen table, yelling at the top of their lungs.

While Dad was unemployed, life became difficult at home. The only money that came in was from Mom's part-time job and a weekly family allowance for the two younger children that came from the government and was paid every Tuesday at our local post office. Whatever unemployment money Dad received, he smoked, gambled, and drank most of it away.

Due to our lacking funds, around Christmas time Mom was forced to appeal to our church for a food basket. This was so demeaning to this proud woman. A man from the St. Vincent de Paul Society visited our home. He apologized to Mom as he checked out our cupboard, but he said he had to ensure that we were truly in need. Since he had attended school with Mom, I know she was mortified to have him search our home.

My Gran Bridget died suddenly in Ireland. When Dad received the telegram, he broke down and cried like a baby. He loved his mother dearly, and they had corresponded regularly. After her death, we never received anymore turkeys for Christmas from Ireland.

Our school was sending underprivileged children for three weeks vacation at a residential school located in Rothesay, a lovely holiday resort in Scotland. It was so exciting and enjoyable for all of us as we stepped aboard the boat for a sail on the River Clyde to our destination. Two teachers were waiting to welcome us. There were two big, stone houses on top of a hill—one for the boys and the other for the girls. I remember we had to climb an abundance of concrete steps to reach the houses, and we slept in twin beds in large dormitories. The houses had lots of big windows and the view of the countryside and the ocean was absolutely breathtaking. A large bathroom had enough bathtubs for everyone, it seemed. The teachers and other staff were very kind to us and we received excellent care. The meals were delicious! In the mornings we had classes and after lunch we were escorted by a pleasant female teacher for a long walk in the countryside, where we often met herds of cows walking along the road. In the evenings we were taught Scottish country dancing to the lovely, Scottish accordion melodies of Jimmy Shand, whom I had often heard play on the radio at home. The three weeks just flew by too quickly.

When I returned home to Govan it was fun relating my holiday stories to my family. How boring to return to my regular lifestyle and school, where the teacher even had homework waiting for me. I seldom got around to doing it, as I was lazy when it came to studying. I was more interested in the latest comic books, school-girl magazines, clothing magazines, and movie stars.

What I really enjoyed was the spelling contest we had once a week at school. A chocolate candy bar and a shiny sixpenny bit were the prize. I will never forget how to spell "woollen" because one week I lost the contest to a boy in my class when I forgot how to spell it. Daydreaming in class, chewing gum, and not paying attention to the teachers were faults that I was punished for many times.

We had our heads checked for lice by the school nurse, but my family never received the dreaded note to take home. This was considered such a disgrace, especially since any children unfortunate enough to have lots of lice, nits, or eggs in their hair had it shaved off. If any of the children had been mean, I would yell "Lousy bug Ha! Ha! Head" at them for my revenge and run away as fast as my legs could carry me.

Our music teacher at school played nice songs on the piano and taught us to sing along. At this time of my life I was very interested in learning to play the piano. My aunt Lilly owned an old piano, and I admired my dear aunt very much as she sat so sedately on her piano seat. Although she played the same classical tunes over and over, they always sounded wonderful to me. We could not afford lessons. Mom told me, "You have nice, long, slender hands and piano fingers," but she thought I had too many big ideas and ambitions. Her remarks did not dent me too much then because I fancied myself as a singer, pianist, and even a dancer on the stage someday. Mom laughed and said, "Oh, Beatrice, the only way you will ever be on a stage will be to scrub it."

The time for me to take the test for entry to high school came when I was twelve. At least half of the boys and girls in my classroom, including me, never did make it to high school. We were placed in secondary school—nicknamed "The Zoo"—which was another building in the same school. I found it most enjoyable because in addition to the usual subjects, we were given physical education and dance classes. The boys had wood shop and science classes, and the girls were taught cooking and baking. Mom had to pay for the ingredients for the delight of the day that I was about to cook or bake. She called them "crookery" classes, and no matter what I made, it was never to her liking. Our class of boys and girls also attended Hills Trust School once a week for art and craft class which I did not enjoy. However, it was a nice walk from St. Anthony's School, and it was great for the talented pupils or would-be artists.

My school friends and I had many fun times. Some of us stuck raisins in our blouses to munch on later. Sometimes they fell out onto the floor, but the teacher did not seem to notice. The best laugh of all was laundry classes. We were requested to take along a different item of clothing to wash and iron each week. The other girls always had clean things to launder, but Mom gave me my dad's dirty shirts, and snotty handkerchiefs. Since we hand washed the clothes by scrubbing them up and down on a small washing board that took the skin off my fingers, I objected to these laundering classes. We used washing soda and washing powder, and the teacher gave me salt to soak the snotty handkerchiefs in before I washed them. She was so squeamish, she made me laugh. Mom assured me that I would make a good laundress some day as I was learning to do it correctly, unlike the other girls who had clean things to wash.

On Fridays we were escorted by our physical-education teacher to the local indoor swimming pool. I learned to swim a little and float, but there was no way I would go into the deep water over my head. I was afraid because once I swallowed a large amount of water and thought I was choking. I played basketball and a game we called net ball, but I excelled in field hockey because I hit my opponents on their shins with the hockey stick.

My cousins Betty and Billy Curren and Maureen Hamilton, who lived at my gran's, often visited our home, but mostly on weekends. They all adored Mom and playing childish games with us. We were always encouraged to play outdoors in good weather, but remained indoors during the bitter Scottish winters. If it merely rained, we went outside, as the rain did not bother us. We were so accustomed to rain we danced through the puddles and played games of tag, kick the can, and even marbles, depending on how heavy the downpour was.

When I visited Gran and Aunt Lilly and Uncle Jimmy, we were told to go out and play to get some fresh air. We enjoyed climbing on top of the roofs of the trash-can enclosures. Gran always kept an eye on us from her kitchen window. Her idea of controlling us was to appear at the window holding a big bread knife up against her neck. "No, no don't do that!" I screamed the first time she did this, as she'd tapped on the window to attract our attention. My cousins were wise to her antics and assured me it was only pretending on her part, and so we just kept on climbing.

One game we played involved placing an old tennis ball inside a ladies' nylon stocking and bouncing it off the walls of the buildings. There was a tower bar next to where Gran lived, so we would bounce the ball and sing our street songs. Some of the words were nasty, but we did not fully realize what they meant.

Whenever we played outside and did not want to go home to eat, we called up to our mothers, "Throw down a jam sandwich!" All the tenement children did this, and our mums wrapped the sandwiches in old newspapers and tossed them out of the windows to us.

We were warned not to talk to strangers. "Be off the streets at 8 AM, noon, and 5 PM," warned our parents. This was when the shipyard whistle went off, and hundreds of men and young, apprentice boys spilled out into the streets. The boys resembled small men, as they all dressed alike in the same work overalls and big, black boots and caps. On Fridays, which were paydays, many of the men went to the bars instead of going home. There were at least eight bars within walking distance from the shipyard. If any child's dad drank heavily, it was understood his wife and family were sadly neglected.

I was really a tomboy, but did not realize it. I owned a big bag full of colored and assorted-sized marbles, which I guarded like pirate's gold. The neighborhood boys treated me like one of them and often called up to my window for me to join them. I'd be all dirty and grimy after kneeling on the ground for long periods of time winning more marbles! My parents were beginning to be annoyed with me, but I figured they were just tough to get along with.

My dear Granmaw suffered from bronchitis every winter. One day when I went to visit her, she was in bed, which seemed unusual to me because she was always busy and had lots of good friends who came to see her. She requested to see my mom because she had not seen her as often as she used to, since Mom was now working both mornings and evenings. The awful shock when Gran died was an ordeal to all of us, and I missed this kind woman dreadfully. She loved me and I adored her. Now I had nobody to tell me how well I looked when I wore my hand-me-down dresses that Mom bought for me off the neighbors. Cousin Maureen went to stay with her dad and stepmother Helen and stepsister Eleanor.

This was a bad time for all the family. The same year Gran died, Dad's only sister, my aunt Sara, died in Ireland. Sara worked hard on the farm in Culleens, Co Sligo, along with her husband Sean. She was expecting twins but the strain was too much on her heart, and she died just as the twins were about due. Dad was out of his mind with grief. The four children she left behind were sent to a children's home. Our only consolation was that we believed our dear aunt Sara went to heaven immediately.

Once a month on Sunday afternoons, Rose, Patricia, Ed, Cousin Betty and I went to the art galleries, which was a pleasant adventure for all of us because it did not cost anything. We sailed across the River Clyde on a ferry boat that also carried cars. When it reached Patrick, we disembarked and then walked up the road to Kelvingrove Park. In summer the River Kelvin and the park were all abloom with flowers, and we could see the Glasgow University building in the distance. Adjacent to the park were the art galleries. We were mesmerized to see so many historical suits of armor, daggers, swords, and shields. There were live snakes under glass, which I did not particularly care for because I was afraid they might escape and bite us. Some of the artwork was lovely, and the huge paintings on the walls were marvels to us all.

Another park we frequented was Bellahouston Park, about a mile from us. Mom assured us, "You will all receive the seven winds, which will be beneficial to your health, but they only blow in Bellahouston Park." I never questioned this because Mom knew best. At Easter time she hard boiled eggs for us and dyed them in cold tea. We delighted in rolling them down the grass hills of the park, believing we could feel the seven winds at our back.

Since our family lived in such cramped quarters, I often overheard my parents talking as they made remarks about two women who lived up the street who apparently drank. I overheard Mom telling Dad that one woman was a secret drinker and the other woman was a closet drinker. I was a curious girl, and one day when Mrs. Tavy was on her way home from shopping, I met her on the street.

"Hello, Mrs. Tavy," I said. "Is a secret really a secret?"

"Oh, yes, deary," she replied.

"Well," I inquired, "if that is true, how come my ma said you are a secret drinker?"

Sometime later I spied Mrs. Gray as she was leaving the butcher's shop. "Hello, Mrs. Gray. Is it not awful dark in the closet when you are drinking tea? My ma said you are a closet drinker!!!"

A local widow woman had a gentleman visitor who arrived on Friday evenings and left on Sunday nights. "Ma," I asked, "who is the man who visits the pretty, blond-haired widow?"

"Oh, he is just her fancy man," she replied, with a note of agitation in her voice.

I could only agree with Mom because this tall, elderly, good-looking man had a clean-cut appearance, and he always wore a gray raincoat with fancy shoulder flaps.

With Dad still unemployed, I got errands to do for the neighbors to try to earn some money for the household. One particular job that paid well was taking items of clothing or jewelry to the pawn shop a few blocks away. I pawned the articles on Monday and then returned on Friday to redeem them again. The only unpleasant thing about going to the pawnbroker's shop was that I would often overhear the person in the next booth. It really upset my heart and stomach to hear some poor woman actually begging the pawn man, whom we all called Uncle, "Please. Just loan me enough money to get my man and the weans their dinner."

Uncle replied, "I told you last time. The shoes are too worn and the is suit stained." The destitute woman would then bow her head, crying, and drag herself out of the shop.

I recall a very conceited girl, about seventeen, who often walked past me as I sat on the windowsill of the ground floor of our building. She looked lovely and so well dressed, hanging on the arm of her boyfriend. I smiled to myself, knowing that her mom would be sending all her clothing to be pawned come Monday. I was the errand girl who would be doing the pawning!

Every few years Mom's sister, my aunt Nora, and Cousin Sandra, visited us from their home in Southampton, England. Aunt Nora resembled my mom, including Mom's good nature, and she baked pies for us. Cousin Sandra was an only child, a pretty blonde who wore nice clothes and spoke so politely and proper in her lovely English accent.

If we were seated for a meal, Cousin Sandra would say, "Excuse me, I have to leave the table." Or if she thought she had offended us, she would apologize, "I'm sorry." We were used to loud, noisy children and although I really loved my cousin, I was very envious of her because she was so different from anyone I had ever met.

Cousin Betty Curren and I were making our confirmation. Before she died, Gran had presented Betty with a treasured gift—her wedding veil to wear while being confirmed. The veil, being so old, was more gray than white, and even the sequins had lost their sparkle. Although I knew Gran would have been proud had she lived to see her wearing it, I thought to myself, "Please God, forgive me for thinking my dear departed Gran's veil looks like an old curtain."

A neighbor of ours, Ruth Burnett, became a Catholic and made her confirmation alongside us. Ruth was a very good-natured person and a very attractive blonde, although a bit overweight. Mom always said, "Skinny people are not as happy as heavy people," which was debatable, as Mom was overweight too!

We were all so happy for Ruth when she married her Irish boyfriend, Barney Travers from Dublin. The Burnett family was not Catholic, but they welcomed Barney with open arms. Ruth's sister, Rachel Donoughy, and her husband and children also lived on our third landing. The elder Burnetts, Mary and Rob and their son Albert, lived on the second landing. Our building had lots of relative-neighbors residing in the flats.

Uncle John, Aunt Annie and our cousins moved out of their crowded tenement home on Neptune Street and relocated out to the suburb of Cardonald into a nice, council house with four bedrooms, a large living room, a cute kitchen, a bathroom, and a back garden. Dad often helped dig and plant in this garden. They were wonderful to visit and always made us welcome. We usually visited every few weeks on

Sunday. Uncle John was a construction supervisor, and Aunt Annie was employed by a thread-mill company in Paisley.

Then there was the rest of the Dowd family. Cousin Jack Dowd, whom I vaguely remember, emigrated to New Zealand when I was very young, and I do not remember him ever coming back to visit. Cousin Chrissy Dowd was always a delightful one. She was thin, pretty, blonde, and vivacious. Day Dowd, yet another cousin, never married. Why he didn't is beyond me, as he was so good looking, with blond hair and blue eyes. He loved to sing Irish songs and worked in construction jobs with my uncle John. He was a catch, for sure!

Other Dowd cousins included Sadie, Vera, Jimmy, Frank, and Nancy. Cousin Sadie seldom visited our home because she was scared of my dad when he was intoxicated—which was often when he was unemployed—so she had good reason to prefer we visit her instead. I remember her as an attractive girl with long, brown hair and blue eyes, who got a nice job as a secretary to a lawyer. Cousin Vera had black hair and gray blue eyes, and she trained to become a hairdresser and emigrated to Toronto, Canada. Jimmy and Frank were dark haired and brown eyed. Jimmy emigrated to Toronto a few years before his sister Vera.

Nancy Dowd visited Glasgow and worked in England for a few years, but her heart was forever in Co Sligo, Ireland. Chrissy had a job in a prestigious ladies fashion shop in the city of Glasgow. She eloped with and married Jim Hughs, an Irishman from County Cavan. Aunt Annie and Uncle John were thrilled because, besides being handsome, their new son-in-law was clean living and did not smoke or drink alcohol of any kind. He was also a hard worker and got a job on construction with my uncle John. The Hughs eventually emigrated to Toronto and returned after a couple of years to live in Scotland.

My dad, on the other hand, must have come from a different fold. Whenever he drank whisky, it affected him more due to his head accident. This was hellish, especially during the cold Scottish winters. Many times we had to jump out of our beds, terrorized out of our wits, wearing only our underwear, and run barefooted upstairs to the third landing and stand there shivering on the cold concrete ground, too scared to even whisper to each other. Too many times I had seen him grab Mom and pin her up against the wall, his hands around her neck, and we worried he would strangle her. She was tough and managed to escape and join us in our misery. Later we all crept silently downstairs to find Dad asleep in bed or in his chair.

I was becoming very resentful, because being the eldest child, Mom depended on me too much and her problems became mine. One time we had the annual 12 July Orange Walk, when certain Protestant people marched in a parade, playing flutes, whistles, drums, and accordions. Dad was out at the bar and as he walked home, he saw the men marching and arrived home in a cranky mood. I remarked to him, "Why go to see the parade if upsets you so much, Da?"

"Oh, I only wanted to see how many of them there was," he remarked. He then proceeded to get green, white, and gold paint and paint our kitchen window and two bedroom windows in the tri-colored pattern of the Irish flag. Although we had a lot of non-Catholic neighbors, they were all wonderful, caring people who sympathized with us in our despair when Dad drank on Friday and Saturday nights and sang with the kitchen window opened wide. Depending on his mood, he sometimes sang Irish songs and half cried when singing a sad Irish martyr song such as "Kevin Barry." Other times he sang nice songs, his favorites including "The Country I'm Leaving Behind," "A Bunch of Violets Blue," and "Londonderry on the Banks of the Foyle."

Chapter 4

Wake Up Call For Da

After my dad fractured his skull, he became moody, especially if he consumed alcohol. Usually it was on Friday and Saturday nights that he drank his preference of double shots of scotch, followed by a black and tan beer chaser. Dad seldom had "the horror," as we children called it, but look out when he did!

Dad saw a donkey or a pony in our kitchen, and we could not disagree because it was real to him. My ma insisted I go along with it and pretend in order to keep Da focused and agreeable. It was okay with me until I got older, but then I objected to having to pretend that there was a pony or donkey in our kitchen and say, "Giddy up, giddy up!" just to humor Dad upon my mom's request, because she put up with it.

A family in our neighborhood moved to "the poor house" for destitute people, and I asked, "Ma, why can't we go there?"

"Because it is the poor house, Beatrice," she retorted.

I yelled back at her, "So what, Ma? Isn't our house a poor house?"

After an absence of eighteen months, Dad returned to his old job at the Foundry. He detested lay-about, lazy people or unemployed men who were able to work and didn't, especially if work was available. Returning to his job was most important to Da.

The thick smoke that we all had to endure came from hundreds of smoking chimneys and fireplaces throughout Govan. Adding insult to injury were the awful smoke stacks of the shipyards and foundries, as the coal that was used was not the smokeless type that was available in later years. This smoke combined with the Scottish fog in the winter and created some of the worst smog imaginable. When I wore a white under-slip, half of it would be soot ridden in no time. I recall there were smog masks that could be bought, yet few people, if any, used them.

Being Catholic, we were encouraged and requested to sacrifice something during Lent, which is the six weeks prior to Easter. My friend Margaret McNally, a lovely girl, quiet and good-natured, with blue eyes, blond hair, and perfect teeth, decided to give up sugar for Lent, and I did likewise. After a few days I gave up the idea and stopped eating sweets instead. Margaret lost so much weight her parents became very concerned. They had her seen by the family doctor, and she was diagnosed with tuberculosis. She was sent away to a special hospital in the lovely Scottish countryside to recuperate.

When we visited her home one day, her mom, whom we called Aunt Mary, complained to my mom that the bedroom was very damp. As I stepped into the bedroom, I could see that the wallpaper was soaking wet and water was seeping in the walls. We only visited Margaret one time while she was in the hospital, and by that time she looked wonderful. When Margaret finally came home, we all were so happy for her and her loving family. We even danced a bit of Irish jig—to the delight of our parents—but we could not keep dancing as we were giggling too much.

Peter McNally was Margaret's brother and the same age as my brother Ed. His ambition was to grow up and join the Royal Navy, following in the footsteps of his uncle who was killed during the war. Their little brother Laurence was too young yet to have any ambitions. Uncle Larry McNally was a very kindly, pleasant man and was employed at the shipyard. Aunt Mary was so loving towards him, and I never heard them say an unpleasant word to each other. Mary would get a basin of water for Larry to soak his feet in after a hard day's work. She would then kneel at his feet and unlace his big, black work boots. She often brushed my hair for me when it was long.

Shortly after Margaret returned from the hospital, the McNally's moved into a council house at House Hillwood, miles away from us. Whenever we visited, Peter let us try on his sailor cap that his grandmother had given to him. Aunt Mary usually fed us eggs and homemade chips that were delicious!

Mrs. McCauley was Aunt Mary's mother. She was a tiny, diminutive woman who also lived in the same Hoey Street tenement building as the McNally's had. Her home was spotless, and it was a pleasure to visit her. She always wore a turban scarf and used snuff, which she carried in a tiny, square box. If she used it in my presence, it made me sneeze. This grand little Irish woman was a widow and although she had lost her husband years earlier and survived the heartbreak of losing her son at sea during the war, she never lost her zest for life. She attended daily mass and was what I considered to be a good Catholic. I truly believe her faith is what kept her going.

All Mom's friends, especially Lizzie and Donny Maxwell, were very kind to us when Dad was unemployed. They made us casseroles and occasionally bought him packs of cigarettes, which were quite expensive.

Bridget in Elder Park (1956).

My life seemed brighter when I got an American pen pal to write to. Brenda was younger than me and lived in Michigan. I enjoyed receiving her interesting letters. Her picture was so cute that my parents remarked, "What a pretty girl." I remember that she wanted to become a lawyer when she grew up. My life seemed so dull compared to hers as we did not have very much in common.

On my birthday Brenda sent me a little, blue, heart-shaped necklace. In the center was a tiny, round piece of glass which, when I looked into it, had "The Lord's Prayer" written on it.

My sisters and brother Ed could not get over it. How did anyone manage to get all that onto a tiny piece of glass? Shortly after receiving this gift, my pen pal and I lost touch with each other. I guess we were too busy growing up.

Aunt Lilly and Uncle Jimmy got divorced, which was no surprise to any of us because he had mistreated her for years and was so jealous of her. My uncle Andy Hamilton, who was Mom and Lilly's brother, was not overly keen on Jimmy from the start. The family always thought she could have done better. However, I liked Uncle Jimmy, as he was always pleasant to me. It was the times, I suppose, and living in overcrowded tenement accommodations did not help matters either.

Uncle Andy was a nice, kind man, but he was in and out of prison many times for petty crimes. He had been an excellent soccer player in his younger days. A bad accident ended this forever, and he had to wear a special boot for his disabled foot. His wife, my aunt Annie, was a very gracious and good-looking woman. Although we seldom saw her, I remember my cousins Peggy, Robert, and Ann.

All of my uncles resembled each other, with the same dark brown eyes and Hamilton black hair. Uncle Marcus was employed as a welder to trade and traveled to different parts of Scotland and England on work assignments. Uncles Robert and Tommy were employed at the shipyard, to the best of my knowledge.

When I was thirteen years old, Mom gave birth to a stillborn baby boy. We kids did not know our mother was even pregnant, since we were ignorant to where babies came from. All we knew was that the "green lady" always carried a bag, and so we innocently assumed there was a baby inside the bag. The midwife nurse wore a green trench coat over her uniform and a green hat, and she carried a good-sized doctor's bag. As Mom was heavyset and wore loose dresses and sweaters, we could never tell whether she had gained or lost any weight. It was an awful shock when Dad awakened us to tell us that Mom had been rushed in an emergency to the hospital in the middle of the night. We had not heard a sound. Apparently my dear mother had worked too many long hours scrubbing rest rooms and office floors on her hands and knees, even scouring ships at times, and the umbilical cord had become entangled around the baby's neck, strangling him. He was baptized Daniel. Dad had to visit the undertaker and get a tiny, white coffin to bury him. The undertaker saw to everything, so I never saw my baby brother or his coffin.

I could just picture my dead baby brother, as Dad described him so well to us. He had a shock of blond, curly hair and blue eyes and was not very big weight wise because he was born two and a half months premature. It would have been lovely to have had another brother, as poor Ed was stuck with four sisters.

Dad was so overwhelmed with grief that he was intoxicated for the entire week that Mom was in the hospital. I stayed home from school to do the chores, and since I was finally becoming a good cook and laundress, this was not a problem. The one thing that I objected to was cleaning up Dad's vomit off our kitchen floor. The wet floor cloths felt so sticky and slippery on my hands from Dad's excrement.

The neighbors were very concerned and stopped by to see if we were all right. When Mom finally came home from the hospital, she was not in a good mood and remained in bed. She really hurt my feelings when she complained that I had spent too much money on food and that the kitchen floor was not scrubbed clean enough. She said, "If anyone comes to the door tell them I am not home."

It so happened that the family doctor, Dr. Lessnoff, came to see her. He was a fine man and a very dear friend to all of us for years. I opened the door and told him, "My mom is not at home."

He pushed past me to get into our flat. "What kind of a lying girl do you have in this house?" he asked my mom.

"Oh, she is only following my orders," she assured him.

One older and wiser neighbor girl tried to convince me how babies were conceived. I was indignant with anger when she informed me that my parents got all of us by doing dirty things to each other. "How dare you," I said. "Not my parents. You are a liar."

I asked Mom if it was true, all the stories I had heard. She was furious and assured me that it was nothing but lies, and I was forbidden to associate or speak to this girl again. Whenever I saw her I would yell, "Ha! Ha! Ha! You are a liar."

My aunt Lilly got remarried to a gentleman named William Montgomery, who been a boarder of Gran's years previously. Although it was fun to visit them, the flat seemed so cold and empty without Gran's presence. Lilly had redecorated and it looked really different. The old, black-iron fireplace was gone and in its place was a tiled fireplace, a new stove and new furniture. They also got a cat.

The 1953 coronation of Queen Elizabeth II was wonderful. The queen was lovely and her husband, the Duke of Edinburgh, was very handsome. The streets of Govan were very colorful as there were flags hanging out of every window. Although every school was closed for this day, each school child was presented with a big, wooden box filled with Canadian apples and received a tin can filled with caramel toffees, with a picture of the queen and duke on the can.

Another big event was when Sir Edmond Hilary conquered Mount Everest. Our entire class of boys and girls was escorted by bus to the city of Glasgow to see the movie of him and his expedition climbing this majestic mountain.

There was an assortment of neighbors in our building. The McDougle family came from the Scottish Highlands, the Isle of Sky, I believe. Mr. and Mrs. McDougle, their son Willy, and daughter Morag were nice people who kept to themselves. The older woman, their mother, often sat outside the entrance to our building.

When Morag McDougle got married, neighbors hung out of windows for a glimpse of the bride, and we kids scrambled to catch the pennies tossed out of the taxi as it sped away. We got confetti all over us, but seldom got any pennies since there were too many kids.

When our friend Kathleen Coleman was about to be married, Rose and I were invited to the party, "The Show of Presents." As was the custom, her friends escorted her to the street, while she wore a paper hat they made from newspaper. We encircled her and sang "Bells Are Ringing For Me and My Gal," "When You're in Love It's the Loveliest Time of Year," and "Daisy, Daisy, Give me Your Answer." We then seated her in a baby's pram and wheeled her into the fish and chips shop for a free take-out meal. After this we pushed her to the ice cream shop for a free cone.

Finally the invited guests—the bridal party, which was her best maid and a bride's maid, a few relatives, and close friends—gathered at the widowed Mom's home. The guests were all women and there were no young girls, my sister Rose and I were the youngest. The very best that could be afforded was served, usually steak pies and peas with tea and sherry and trifle desert. We were then taken into the bedroom to see to the bride-to-be's presents, which were practical gifts: cutlery, linen, bedding, towels, dishes, pots, and pans. We did not attend the wedding, only the before party.

Mrs. Lilly was a widow who lived on the third landing along with her daughter, Janet, and her son, Hugh. The children were older than me, and Mrs. Lilly often gave my mother clothing of Janet's for me to wear. They were really nice hand-me-down clothes. Mom did not usually have to pay for them, but I do recall receiving a tartan kilt which Mom purchased. She assured me, "It will keep you warm for many a cold winter. It's a good hap for you to wear."

A large number of our neighbors were relocated to bigger council homes away in the suburbs of Pollock, Nitshill, Priesthill, Househillwood, Castlemilk, and other housing developments. However the rents were steep, and a lot of people found it difficult to pay. "It'd be wonderful," I used to think, "they all got gardens and a bathroom now, and a bathtub."

My family was also on the housing list, and we were always hoping to get a bigger home.

My parents engaged a lawyer to handle a claim for Dad's work accident, and Dad finally received a cash settlement. As Dad had apparently borrowed money from his lawyer, his cash settlement was not as large an amount as it should have been. He gave half of the money to Mom, and to my surprise, I was given a bank book with one hundred pounds deposited in my name. I always said, "When I grow up, I am going to emigrate to America."

The settlement arrived in time for Christmas, and we were overjoyed because we got our very first Christmas tree. The tree was two feet tall, and Dad put it on top of a small table next to the bedroom corner window. We all helped to trim it, and the twinkling lights were dazzling! We were also given presents of new clothing and the younger children got toys. Violet received a toy puppy dog that could be pushed along on its wheels. I remember that she was terrified of it at first, and so we took turns pushing it along and around the kitchen table until our little sister became assured it was her toy and would not hurt or bite her. We were amused watching her. Although she appeared to be afraid of dogs for some reason, eventually she enjoyed her gift.

Da and Bridget

My parents also bought all new furniture. We got a stereo, which was also a nice piece of furniture since the stereo was inside a polished cabinet, and records to play on the stereo. My parents new bedroom furniture consisted of a large ladies' wardrobe and smaller gents' wardrobe, each with a door.

We girls got two new double beds, and Patricia got a small single bed. Patricia didn't like it because she preferred to sleep with us in the one double bed, but it was great having two double beds since there were five of us in the one bed now that Cousin Betty was living with us. Brother Edward got a new single bed, which meant there were six of us in one bedroom, but we were okay, as that's the way it was.

The following spring Dad, our former boarder Joe Whitaker, and I set off on a trip to Roslea in County Sligo, Ireland, to visit his father and other relatives. The three of us set sail from Broomilaw, in Glasgow, and we enjoyed our overnight boat trip. Since we only ate a light supper, I do not recall any one of us getting seasick. Dad had purchased a new radio to take to his family in Ireland, which was packed inside a big box and very awkward to handle. After our long journey by sea and bus, we finally reached our destination. It seemed awfully strange returning to my grandparent's home to find no Granmaw there, just her big empty chair by the glowing turf fireside. Grandda looked the same as I remembered him to be, yet he seemed older in some way. I believe the loss of Gran took quite a toll upon him. Uncle Jimmy and Cousin Nancy had a warm Irish welcome for us.

The radio was the main attraction, and the neighbors came to hear it. Since they lived in such a remote area, not too many, if any of them, had radios. After a good night's rest, I was revived the following morning. I tried to recall my earlier haunts from when I had lived in Ireland for a year as a little, seven-year-old girl. The weather was nice in the month of March, but chilly. The walk to the river was enjoyable, and I delighted in putting my bare feet into the cold water and sitting on a big stone for an hour.

The family liked old Joe, especially my grandda, who really enjoyed chatting to him as the two of them walked about the farm. One day, while the relatives were entertaining Joe, Dad and I walked to the ocean to see the O'Dowd castle. Together we climbed up through the ruins of the old place, and waded into the sea, where the rocks felt slippery, mossy, and full of seaweed. Dad cavorted like a young boy, with his pant legs rolled up to his knees. He brought along a small, sharp knife and cut periwinkles and mussels off of the rocks. When he had a bucket half filled, he ordered me, "Go and wait on the sand for me while I try to get some dulce seaweed," which he claimed was also beneficial to one's health.

I was amazed to get these shellfish for free. At home in Govan, there was a man who sold periwinkles out of a wheelbarrow. He would come around the streets yelling "Pennies for Whelk's Periwinkles," and the people gladly paid him. In return, we received a good helping, wrapped up in newspapers with a tiny pin to dig them out of their shells.

I was prepared for this trip to the ocean side, and had taken a pin along with me. While I was waiting for Dad, I began to eat the periwinkles from the bucket. When he returned, I complained, "Da, these Irish shellfish are too tough to remove from their shell, and hard to chew."

He looked startled, "Don't tell me you have eaten any of them, Beatrice?"

"Oh, yes, Da," I replied. I did not realize that they were raw and had to be boiled in water before they were edible. No wonder they were so tough—they were alive! I almost vomited on the spot.

Cousin Nancy boiled the shellfish in a big, black, iron pot as I sat by the turf fireside waiting. The kitchen was so cozy, and the smell of turf burning smelled so nice. We enjoyed the shellfish for dinner, along with mashed potatoes. There were two dogs, and they begged us for potato skins, while the cats remained outside close to the cow shed.

The following day I was so sick with a stomach ache and diarrhea-like dysentery. When it had eased off a little, Dad borrowed Uncle Jimmy's bicycle, and Cousin Nancy loaned me her bicycle. We set off on a cycling ride to pay a visit to my Uncle Frank, who lived in Clooney, just a few miles from Grandda's home. They were discussing my problem, and my uncle decided that I should try and drink a clear liquid he had on hand. It looked like lemonade to me, and I drank a good mouthful of it. I immediately felt the warmth of it as it went to my stomach and almost down to my toes, so it seemed.

Meanwhile, Uncle Frank and Dad were having a good time drinking and talking about old times gone by. We did not leave until late that night, and I remember there was a bright, full moon. We were cycling quickly downhill on our way home Grandda's. Da was in front of me as we reached the end of a narrow road, where there was a big gate. I watched him topple over the handlebars of his bicycle and over the gate into the big field, and I yelled, "Da, are you all right?" He jumped up off the ground, got on his bicycle, and away we went to Grandda's. The bottle of potsheen, homemade brew, in his back pocket was still intact. Da did not lose a drop of its precious contents, which he called "the cure!"

The next day I was completely better. A few relatives and neighbors stopped by to visit, and since old Joe was originally from Dublin, he fit in perfectly. It was heartwarming to watch the men filling their pipes with tobacco and puffing away as they conversed with each other. Dad and Uncle Jimmy smoked cigarettes and occasionally Dad smoked a pipe. They sat in kitchen chairs around the front of the turf fireside, conversing. I enjoyed the smell of sod, turf peat, and smoking pipes.

Dad's favorite tobacco was walnut plug. He and Ma used to argue about the expense caused by extravagant smoking habits, so he switched from cigarettes to pipe. But then he smoked both, which was twice as costly!

We missed Gran's presence. Our vacation ended too quickly, and we said our good-byes and boarded the bus for Londonderry, in Northern Ireland. The journey was long, yet pleasurable. Our bus driver stopped at villages along the way to chat with the local people, drop off a package, or pick one up. I enjoyed gazing out of the window at the cattle grazing in fields that seemed to have many assorted shades of green. When the bus reached Donegal, the driver informed all of the passengers it was break time, so Dad went into the bar for a few pints of beer, while Joe and I enjoyed tea and sandwiches for our half-hour rest.

The bus driver returned, and he waited for Dad until he could not delay any longer, so we left without him. Joe and I were at our wits end with worry because Dad had our return tickets for the boat ride home to Glasgow. No worries! Dad hired a car and driver to catch up with the bus. What a relief!

We had time to spare before the boat sailed, so we did a little walking to see The Walls of Derry. The concrete walls were engraved with figures of William of Orange and his soldiers fighting the Seventeenth century Battle of the Boyne, which they won. We finally boarded the boat and all of us got a little seasick as the boat sailed across the Irish Sea and into Glasgow.

Mom was pleased to have us home again. The latest news was that she was about to start working full-time in a new job at the cooperative furniture factory. This was not a problem because my youngest sister Violet was starting school. We were delighted to have Mom home at breakfast time. She also came home by bus around noon to feed us all our dinner, which she prepared the night before and therefore only needed re-heating. I was very willing to do any chores after school ended at 4 PM and have a warm fire started for Mom's arrival home shortly after 5 PM. One night a week, she was required to work until 8 PM. Her job was filling cushions with foam rubber and sewing them closed. She was also responsible for checking the sofas and chairs for any flaws before they were transported by truck to the stores. The job gave her a new outlook on life, and she made lots of friends. It meant more freedom for me, because she was home most evenings to make Dad's supper.

On Monday evenings Dad would reluctantly attend a movie with Mom, who always wore a hat. On Tuesdays Ma worked late, and when she got off at 8 PM, she went to the late show movies with her friend and supervisor in the sewing department, Margaret Harte.

Ma would leave instructions on what to cook for dinner. On one occasion I was to boil cabbage, and she said to put baking soda in to make it tender. It turned out brown, and she was furious. She forget to tell me how much soda—just a pinch—and I'd put in half a cup.

A co-worker of Mom's sold her an almost-new lady's bicycle, which was a lovely surprise for me. My first bicycle ever—and I was over the moon with delight! On weekends a neighbor, May Baily, and I enjoyed many cycling trips around the lovely countryside of the River Clyde. I was a bit of a fanatic with my bike and spent endless hours polishing it. My cousin Betty, who was now living at our home, enjoyed riding the bike. She was a blue-eyed, blonde, pretty girl, and one day, while riding my well-maintained bicycle, she fell off. I was absolutely furious! How dare she fall off my new bike! As poor Betty was half sitting, stunned after hitting her forehead on the ground, I ran over and promptly picked up my bike to examine it while Betty apologized for falling off of it!

Dad had many friends he met on his bar crawls and he was also very popular at work. One of his friends was Tom Kennedy, a very handsome Irishman with jet black, wavy hair and sea blue eyes. His wife was sickly and always in the hospital. They had a son named Teddy. After a lengthy illness Mrs. Kennedy died. When Tom came to our home for sympathy, Mom cooked him scrambled eggs with grated cheese inside, brewed a big pot full of tea, and baked buttered bread for him. Since Tom had not eaten a meal all day, he really appreciated it.

Sometime later an Irish family was managing one of the news agent shops on Golspie Street, near our home. The two women who worked there were sisters, Delia Mahon and her sister Annie. Dad frequented this shop, buying newspapers and cigarettes. He decided to become a matchmaker and introduced Tom Kennedy to Annie. Eventually they were married, and Dad was the best man. We were all elated because we wanted Tom to be happy and not lonely, and Teddy would have a nice stepmother to care for him.

Annie had a brother John, who came over from Ireland to work on the subway underground train at Govan Cross. Although he enjoyed his job and liked Glasgow and its friendly people, John missed his farm life in Ireland. After working for a few years he returned to live there. It was not unusual for people to be homesick. People returned to Ireland to care for ailing parents or to marry. Some returned to the farm or because they were just plain dying to go back home.

Mom decided to take the five of us on a vacation to visit her cousins in County Tyrone in Northern Ireland. Our cousin Betty Curren decided that she would join us, and a neighbor of ours, Kathy Coleman, also came along. Dad was only too happy to see us off, since he would have a quiet home to live in for a change. We enjoyed our train ride from Glasgow Central Station to a place called Ardrossen. There was a ship waiting to take us and the other passengers on a four-hour daylight sail to Belfast, the capital of Northern Ireland. We had a fun time on the boat, and we enjoyed a lunch of fish and chips.

When we arrived in lovely Northern Ireland, we traveled by bus to Ballinderry Bridge, which took a few hours. What a tiring journey! I slept the whole way. When the bus stopped, Mom hired a taxi to take us to Cousin Annie McKeever McElhone's home in the countryside. The unpaved roads were covered in small, loose stones.

After a bumpy ride, we reached our cousins' cottage, and they were delighted to see us. Annie was an elderly widow who lived with her old brother, Patrick, and her two sons, Gerry and Patrick, who were in their twenties. The men were all bachelors. Annie lived in a nice, thatched, pleasant-smelling cottage that had a good-sized kitchen with a big, black, cast-iron, pot-bellied range that was used for heating and cooking. Annie was a wonderful cook and baker and a spotless housekeeper. When she made griddle scones on top of the black, cast-iron range, we ate them up as quick as she could make them. The fresh country air gave us good appetites. She remarked, "You act as if you were starved."

There were two big bedrooms on opposite sides of the kitchen. The bedroom we slept in contained two large, comfortable double beds and a twin bed for Annie. The cottage had no indoor plumbing or electricity.

We spent most of our days picking blackberries and raspberries. Annie sent my brother Ed and me to fetch pails of water from the neighbors Patrick and Lena McVey's spring well. To get to their cottage, we walked about a quarter mile down a quiet, country road and up another long, narrow, boreen road. My brother and I were in no hurry, and so we often stopped to talk to the many animals grazing in the fields. One day we went into a field to check for blackberries and a big, black bull chased us. I got to the gate first and yelled to my brother, "Come on, run faster!" Thankfully he just made it to the gate on time.

From a distance we could hear Annie calling to us, "Come home, boy, come home, girl," because she needed the water to make her tea or for drinking. For bathing and washing clothes, she collected rainwater in a tall barrel underneath the thatched roof of the cottage, and it was so soft.

On one of our daily travels to get water, we heard violin music, and being curious kids, we followed the direction it came from. There was not another person or thing in sight—just a big, empty field, and on the grass was a big circle of shorter grass. We continued on our way for the water, and on our way back we stopped off at the same field. We stood amazed because the grass was now all the same length—not a trace of a circle. When we arrived back at the cottage, all excited and with half of the water spilled, everyone was waiting for their tea and they were not overly happy with us for taking too long. No one paid any attention to our story, and to this day I do not know who cut the lawn or played the beautiful music.

The couple who owned the well were very friendly, and they had a little baby, too. They talked to us, and I think they enjoyed hearing our Glaswegian accent. We had overheard that Patrick McVey was in bad health, and so I asked him if it was true. "You look so well," I told him. Indeed he was a good-looking, pleasant man. Patrick smiled at me and replied, "Yes, Beatrice, it is true. There is something wrong with my blood cells." My brother and I assured him he looked good to us, and he really did.

When we returned to the cottage and told Mom and Annie about our conversation they were annoyed at us. "You should be minding your own business and not be meddling in grown-up matters," they scolded.

We seldom saw Annie's two sons, Gerry and Patrick, or Annie's brother Patrick as they were gone all day working on neighbors' farms. However, Patrick used soot for polishing his teeth, and when he smiled his big, toothy grin, we laughed. The McKeever's farm was small, and they grew flax, as did most everyone, I believe. The men and women worked very hard as the work was back-breaking labor. They pulled the tall, grass-like, tough flax with their bare hands, and even when it caused their hands to bleed, they kept on working the fields. When the flax was all pulled from the fields, it was then soaked in a big stream of water for weeks, and the stench that came off it was awful!

I recall the Donnelly family had two sons. One of them was a priest, and he helped too. It was most unusual for me to see a priest up to his waist in stinking water removing smelly flax. When I told him this, he laughed loudly. The flax was then spread out on the grass to dry. Once it was harvested, the flax was tied together in bunches and shipped by donkey cart to the nearby Hardy's Mill for scrunching and then shipped to the mills in Belfast to be made into linen.

Annie sent us with big cans of tea and her delicious Irish bread to feed the many workers in the fields. This was a fun time for all of us city children. The neighbors were wonderful people, and we made friends with them and their children. They were Protestant and Catholic, all working together. On 12 July, the Protestants held their march to commemorate a seventeenth century victory, Battle of the Boyne. The Catholics held a holiday march on 15 August. These people got along so well together, they borrowed musical instruments off each other to play in their parades.

Mom was enjoying herself visiting other cousins in Ballougherty, the McCuckins. They always invited her with the expression, "Come visit with us, Rosy. Your name is on the teapot."

Rose, Patricia, and Violet did not wander all over the fields like my brother Ed and me. The cleg flies and midgies were a nuisance and for some reason they liked us, especially Patricia—they bit her unmercifully.

When Annie McKeever McElhone attended a Saturday night dance, she would be in a very good mood on Sunday. After attending mass, she had the dinner all ready in the oven, and then the fun began. She would start to hum an Irish dance tune and proceed to dance an Irish hornpipe all around the kitchen floor. We clapped and yelled to encourage her to keep on dancing. Her breasts also danced and bounced up and down, as she was well endowed.

Annie's two sons Gerry and Patrick were becoming restless and thinking about emigrating to Canada. Gerry owned a greyhound racing dog that he kept in a shed, especially if it was due to race. Beauty was black and white, a truly beautiful animal. We could hear it whimpering behind the closed door of the shed. "Don't feed it anything," we were told. But we placed scraps of leftover meals we had saved for the dog underneath the door, and we could hear the shlop, shlop of the dog devouring it up. The dog won races, despite our feeding it.

Whenever Annie needed something from the store, she let us use her new bicycle to go fetch these items, as the store was a fair distance away from the cottage. Kinnears sold almost everything and also served as the local post office. The owners were very friendly. Many times we children went walking there to buy post cards to send home to friends and relatives and also to buy treats.

Several nights a week visitors would arrive at the cottage to play music on the accordion and the whistles. They played traditional Irish songs, and we all sang along and told silly jokes. There was no alcohol allowed, so the visitors enjoyed tea, cookies, and Irish bread. As the night progressed the visitors told ghost stories. My parents were inclined to be superstitious, and I believed in ghosts. I got so scared, and after the visitors left, I became shivery and nervous. The tiny, red flickering of the kerosene lamp on the Sacred Heart picture and the almost dark kitchen was eerie. As we crept into bed, it seemed as if all the religious pictures that hung in the bedroom and the statues were watching us.

Like my Irish grandparents, the McKeever's used kerosene oil lamps for light. They were called "tilly lamps" and looked like small lantern lamps. Amazingly, the light of these lamps was as good as electric light. They used a little wick called the mantle, which was so flimsy it was almost like ashes. If you touched it, it disintegrated. Cousin Annie was very annoyed whenever she had to replace it and always demanded, "Who done it?" Me, of course. I was a curious girl.

My brother and I had picked so many blackberries that we had enough to sell. Ed was so pleased, and he decided that I should hold the money to buy small gifts. His share was for safekeeping until a later date.

Annie introduced us to the Devlin family, who lived in nearby Ballygillen. There were so many people with this name that this family was known as the white-haired Devlin's. Dorothy, who was English, and her Irish husband, Joe, were farmers and very wonderful people. Their large family of good-looking, blue-eyed, blonde children was a sight to behold. While walking to mass on Sundays, we often met them on the road, and they were so clean and well dressed. I liked all the brothers and sisters, but especially Tony. Tony was the eldest child, a tall, quiet, and good-looking boy who often stopped by to see us. Annie said he really came to see me, but I did not believe her since I was not used to boys liking me or paying the least attention to me.

Annie's cottage in Ballymoyle was so remote, few cars passed by, and instead we mostly saw cyclists. Annie had an annoying habit that irked me. If a person walked past the cottage, and she missed seeing who it was, she gave me a slap on the back and told me to run and look. When I returned, I had to describe whatever the person was wearing until she was satisfied. If I did not catch a glimpse of them in time, she became agitated.

After a wonderful, refreshing vacation we finally returned home to Scotland. When we arrived in Govan we found our flat a mess. Dad had left a pail of smelly, moldy cans and dirty dishes in the sink. He was in a pouty mood, complaining that there was no one to take care of him. However the neighbors informed us that he had lived it up while we were on vacation. He ate at fine restaurants and gave big tips to the waitresses.

The cat was missing, and Dad said it had run away, probably to look for us. I could feel a sense of dread in my heart because I remembered the time when I was a little girl and we had a cat called Minny. One morning I awoke to see about six adorable kittens, so tiny and fluffy, barely fitting into my hand. "Please can we keep them? Even one?" I begged Dad.

He retorted, "We can not afford them." I followed him to our toilet and watched him flush the helpless kittens one by one.

There was also a memory of the time Dad had arrived home from his work for his noon dinner. He was carrying a big, orange cat and insisted that this was the cat that had been pooping on our wooden doorstep. He ordered Ed and me to hold the cat's legs while he castrated it with a razor blade. The cat was so terrified it never made a sound. The cat survived but when he saw Dad, he ran so fast you could not see him for the dust.

My three sisters and my brother were precious to me. Twelve year-old Ed, the second oldest, passed his high school entry test, receiving top marks, and went to St. Gerard's High School. We were all so proud of him. Rose, the third oldest in the family, was now ten years old and getting chubby. Patricia was growing up to be noticeably pretty, but was still a thin, delicate child. Ed and I were envious of the way she demanded and received lots of attention from Mom. Violet was a curly-haired, happy child of five years who enjoyed school and all her little friends.

CHAPTER 5

Bridget Growing Up

As for me, at age fourteen I was still a tom-boy. Around this time, I noticed that most of the girls in my classroom at school were developing breasts, but I did not have anything noticeable. The newspapers and magazines were advertising creams that were supposed to enlarge the breasts, and I pleaded with Mom to get this magic cream. She replied, "All in good time, Bea. Do not rush growing up."

To keep me quiet, she bought me my first bra, a pink one, at the Glasgow Gallowgate from the Barras, a second-hand place that was very popular and busy, especially on Saturdays. To enhance my neglected upper torso I placed two of Mom's old nylon stockings inside each cup, and I was very pleased with my appearance. The following Monday morning, I was passing out pencils to my fellow classmates. I could see that the boys were noticing me, and I thought to myself, "Now I look developed and important."

My odd-errand jobs meant extra cash for me, and I attended the cinema regularly. There were four cinemas within walking distance from my home: The Elder, The Lyceum, The Plaza, and The Vogue. My favorite was The Lyceum because it was always clean and spotless, and even the rest room was a pleasure to visit. A uniformed door man always seemed to be there, and he was pleasant. Sometimes while waiting in line, we were entertained by a very talented accordion player.

When I returned home, my sisters and brother Ed were eagerly waiting for me, already in bed, because it would be after 10:30 PM. I related the story of the movie to them and you could hear a pin drop, they listened so attentively. If it was a sad movie, I could hear them sniffle. An amusing comedy movie made them laugh loudly, and Mom often appeared in our bedroom brandishing the broom. She would give us a good whack with the broom and say, "I know it is that Beatrice," and proceed to whack who she thought was me. We hid our heads underneath the bed covers. Since I usually had moved, quite often it was one of my sisters who received the brunt of the broom.

We were all growing up by now and getting along in harmony with each other. Attending secondary school was most enjoyable for me, and

The Dowd family growing up (1960): Patsy, Ma, Da, Rose and Violet.

I really loved the gym classes and also the dance classes. I had a few nice school friends myself, although I missed my primary-school friends who made it to high school, Roseann Stevenson and Mary Feeley. Roseanne had ambitions of becoming a school teacher. I never saw them again.

Ena Gunn attended secondary school and sat beside me in class. She was a very amusing girl, and we giggled a lot in class. Once I went to secondary school, I was never punished with the awful tause belt, and I must say it was great.

I also had street friends whom I always saw, and some from the other streets. Alice Wilson was from Garmouth Street; Jeanette

McKlerny was from Elder Street, and Eva Kay lived on Fairfield Street, which was my street.

Swimming lessons were fun, too. If it was a cold winter's day, and I knew I would be freezing while walking home for my noon dinner, I would make an excuse to the teacher, "I have my illness." This was the excuse the other girls gave, and all I understood was that whatever this awful illness was, they dare not go into the water. I would look at the girls and think, "They don't look sick."

Finally one day the teacher remarked to me, "Miss Dowd, is it not strange that you seem to have your illness every second week and sometimes every week?" I hinted to my parents about this illness that my classmates had, but they did not show any interest. I did not have the nerve to ask my friends, since I was supposed to be a smart person, but I obviously was ignorant about this.

My street friends were now adding other games to their list. One in particular was "chase and catch kiss." The girls ran through to the back courts of the tenements with the boys in pursuit. If any boy caught up with a girl, she had to allow him to kiss her. I was not too keen on this idea. All I knew was that the boys ran past me, even when I became tired and ran slowly. "Why is this?" I complained to my parents. They did not tell me, and I remained in a fog over the entire issue.

Mom was very popular at her work and she made many friends. She entertained them on Friday evenings, usually the same crowd: Margaret and James Harte, Sylvia Ross, Isabell Crighton, who was Willy Crighton's daughter (Willy was the boss at the furniture factory, and a fair and pleasant person to work for), Lizzy and Donny Maxwell and sometimes Mary McNally. They all enjoyed visiting our home, and sang and talked late into the night. The Harte's were childless, but they adopted the five of us into their hearts. Dad usually arrived home late on Friday, and depending on his mood, these good people would humor him and encourage him to sing.

Late one Saturday night Mom was awakened by Dad. He had a guest with him whom he wanted Mom to meet. The guest was a Chinese man named Wong Kin Yin. He was about forty years old and employed on a ship that had arrived recently from a far-away land. I think he was employed as a ship's cook. Wong became a frequent visitor to our home and always stopped by whenever his ship was docked nearby.

Wong gave Dad some curry powder and assured him it was beneficial to our health. Dad insisted we try some, so he sprinkled it all over our dinner! It was hot and made us sneeze. There was no way we were ever going to eat that stuff again.

When I was fourteen and a half, I went to the toilet one evening and discovered I was bleeding. I was very concerned and ran to Mom crying, "Oh, Ma, am I going to die?"

She was not overly helpful and just said, "The bleeding will occur every four weeks. Here is some money to get some sanitary pads at the drug store. Keep yourself clean and stay away from the boys."

The boys were my friends. "What did they have to do with this happening to me?" I wondered. I became a fanatic about cleanliness, and I used to imagine that the boys knew it was that time of the month and could smell me.

Once a week I was sent to the local public baths, as we did not have a tub in our apartment. The baths were located in the same building as the swimming pool, and the men's baths were separate from the women's. A woman attendant would run a hot bath for me. I had half an hour to get undressed, bathe, dry myself, and get out. If I was enjoying the bath too long, she hammered on the door yelling, "Time's up! Come on! Get out!" It cost twelve pennies to have a bath, and it was worth it.

One summer evening, I was wearing a sleeveless blouse, and my dad spotted my hairy underarm pits and decided it was time my arm pits were shaved. He told me to stand near the kitchen window and hold my arms up while he shaved them, using his shaving brush, soap, and his razor. "It's high time you had under your oxters shaved." After this ordeal, Mom bought me a tiny ladies' razor so I could do this for myself.

Now I realized that the chemist shop was not just for medicine, but it sold lots of items for girls– perfume, perfume lozenges for sweetening one's breath, fancy soaps, lipsticks, and haircurlers. I wished I could be beautiful like the movie stars and have pretty clothes, too. I dreamed of a nice, big house with my very own bedroom, and ice cream anytime.

My cousin Betty was a good-natured lassie, and I often went to her mother's home on Sunday afternoons. This was always a good day to visit since we knew my aunt Lilly would be out walking, she enjoyed a walk in the Elder Park. Lilly was an unusually striking woman. She had long, black hair, a trim figure, and was always fashionably dressed, even if in second-hand clothing. I often wondered why she didn't just let her hair hang loose instead of pinning it on top of her head, all wrapped in a roll so prim and proper. Anyway, Aunt Lilly used good make-up, which Betty and I enjoyed putting on our faces. We hoped Aunt Lilly would not notice that we had been messing with her cosmetics while she was out walking. If she noticed, she never mentioned it.

My sister Rose was a popular girl and made friends easily. Two of her best friends were Marcella DeLoria and Isabell Campbell, both very nice girls. Marcella had black hair and dark eyes and was very sincere, sensible, and smart. Isabell was devilish and full of fun. She had brown hair and eyes. She did a great impersonation of a wonderful singer, Eartha Kitt, singing "An Old-Fashioned Millionaire." My ma would be in stitches, and even Dad smiled. Yes, Isabel was a delight because she could make people laugh.

Bridget, Da, and Violet.

Now that we were getting older, my parents allowed us to have friends visit on occasion. I never saw my brother's pals. Maybe Ed was intimidated being the only boy, but I do recall that one evening a friend of Ed's came to our door. When Dad answered the knock, a boy stood there and inquired, "Is Dowdy coming out?"

Dad replied, "I am afraid you have the wrong home; there is no Dowdy living here." As Ed was waiting for his friend, he was not too pleased with Dad for sending him away. However, Dad informed my brother that our name was Dowd not Dowdy.

One day a letter arrived from Ireland from Uncle Danny, who had written to tell us to expect a visitor from Sligo named Anthony Kilcauley. I got the job of staying home from school to welcome him to Glasgow. At 8:30 AM I heard the door, and when I opened it a tired-looking young man stood there holding a small, brown, worn, leather suitcase.

"Come on in," I said. "I am Beatrice, and I am going to make your breakfast." He appeared to be shy and only talked if I asked him questions. After he ate his breakfast he seemed more at ease. I was kind of sorry for him, as he sat so dejected looking beside the fireplace in our kitchen. "Do you have any good reading books in your suitcase?" I asked.

"Yes," he replied and opened the suitcase. A pile of small religious books fell out onto the floor. By the time my parents and the rest of the family arrived home around noon for dinner, I knew he was twenty-one and liked to be called Tony. Dad was delighted to have one of his countrymen visit him, and since Tony came from outside of Easkey, a place called Clan Easkey—I believe it was—this was even better. My parents arranged accommodation for Tony at Mrs. McCauley's home, and Dad arranged employment for him almost immediately. He was grateful to my parents and visited our home every week.

Our neighbor Kathy Coleman was five or six years older than me and was employed at the Galbraith's bakery factory. When I left school at the age of fifteen, she was instrumental in getting me employment working beside her in the snowball department. I was so excited the Monday I was to start my very first job. I met Kathy before 7 AM and we walked the three-quarters of a mile to the factory. A nice lady gave me a snow white uniform and a white turban to cover my hair.

The snowball department was so clean. There were big, wooden tables and at least eight young women employed there, including May Baily, another neighbor I went on cycling trips with. The girls trained me to stick two small cakes together with jam and place them into a large, wooden tray board until it was filled. The next step was for Kathy to dip them in melted icing sugar. They were returned back to us, and we proceeded to roll them in coconut flakes. Appropriately named "snowballs," the finished sweets were placed into the tray boards, which were heavy and awkward to lift. There was an art to this, and I quickly learned to lift them onto my shoulder and put them into the shelves of a large, stainless-steel cart. Finally I wheeled the cart to the elevator, where they were taken to the ground floor, loaded on waiting trucks, and then delivered to the bakery stores where the snowballs were sold.

We stood working at long, wooden tables. The men supervisors were strict but kindly and saw to it that we were treated fairly. We got our regular, timed breaks, since the work whistle went off at break time and quitting time. There was also a very good cafeteria that sold cheap-priced meals to the employees. Before finishing at 4 PM, we all helped scrub off the equipment, tables, and floors with long, wooden-handled scrubbers. The bakery smelled so good and it was always spotlessly clean. It was a pleasure for me to go to work instead of school, even though I had to get out of my bed by 6 AM to start work at 7:15 AM (I got the extra fifteen minutes grace until I was sixteen years of age).

I think Mom was proud of me. I remember rushing home to present her with my very first, unopened wage envelope. She gave me an allowance out of it, and I thought I was well off and on my way to being independent. I was a good, fast worker but the wages were paid by age. Since I was only fifteen, I received much less then the older women employees. Thus no matter how much or how hard I worked I always received very little for my efforts.

Before the Christmas season I was transferred temporarily to the currant-cake department, where there was a high demand for the delicious currant and fruit cakes. A neighbor, Rachel Donoughy, worked in this department.

I always believed people should live forever, and the childish part of me became numb with grief whenever anyone I cared for died. Old Trigs became ill, and as her health deteriorated, I could overhear her crying and wailing in the night, "Oh, God, what will happen to wee David?" This wonderful woman, whom I had grown to love, was not concerned about herself. She knew she was dying, and yet what she worried about was her grandson's welfare.

When Trigs finally passed away, Dad insisted we pay our respects. She laid dead in her bed, but to my surprise she looked like she was asleep. We all said a prayer for the repose of her soul. We were certain she went to Heaven, while David went to live with relatives.

My bakery job was going well, and I was content to have a job. I still helped with chores at home, and I actually enjoyed housework. Dad often remarked that cleaning and cooking would do me no harm and that I would make a good wife for somebody someday. I thought to myself, "That's what you think, because I am never getting married." I decided I would never marry anyone to become a drudge like my mother was. My da could not even fetch his own socks or underdrawers. He'd yell, "Rosetta, Rosetta. Where's me clean drawers . . . me tay . . . dinner . . . hanky?" And I'd mutter under my breath, "Where's me arse?" and Ma got mad at me for swearing.

It seemed strange not to wear ankle socks anymore. Nylon stockings were expensive and tore easily, and so they were kept for weekends or special occasions only. Whenever I wanted a new dress or shoes I saved a little each week until I had enough to pay for them. My parents did not allow me to wear makeup, but finally relented to my pleas to wear lipstick and perfume.

Slim skirts with side slits were in fashion, and a few of my friends were wearing them. No matter how often I pleaded with my parents to get their permission to purchase one, the answer was a definite, "No!"

"That's not for you, Bea. Stop trying to copy people," they would remark.

One day as I was walking home from work, I saw a notice in the beauty-parlor window that read, "Get the D.A. haircut." My hair was long and wavy at this time, but I had seen a picture of a popular movie star with this haircut, and I wanted to look like her. After it was cut I went home, confident that I looked pretty. When I arrived home Mom was not too upset with me. It was a Friday, and Dad was a little late arriving home and was also tipsy. He laughed at me as I tried to explain my new hair style, which was quite short and also feathered at the back. "Indeed it is a D.A.," he told me, "A duck's ass." It had not occurred to me what D.A. meant. My dad decided that my new haircut was uneven and not an asset to my appearance. So, against my wishes, he placed a bowl on top of my head and chopped my hair off. I was so ashamed to be seen in public that I wore a head scarf whenever I went outside.

My friend Margaret McNally and I often attended a movie on Friday evenings. We bought chocolate bars and candy, and I had tried smoking cigarettes. However, I did not want to become addicted, so I only bought one or two cigarettes on Friday. Yes, one could buy a single cigarette way back then. The most popular brand was called Coffin Nails. Smoking was allowed in the cinema, and there were tiny ash trays attached to the seats. If the movie was exciting, my friend's job was to light my cigarette. I took a few puffs, and then extinguished it to be re-lit several times during the show. After a while I gave up on cigarettes—they only made me dizzy anyway!

A young man at Mom's work had been a Navy cook, and he was looking for a girl to accompany him to a Navy-related dinner and dance party he had been invited to. Paddy was the man's name, and he was an upholsterer by trade. I protested, "Ma, I do not know this person." She assured me that he was very nice, and she even borrowed a dress and necklace for me to wear from our friend Mary Glasgow, who also worked alongside Mom at the furniture factory.

Bridget and Paddy at the dinner dance.

Since I had not yet dated anyone, I was more than a little nervous as my family and I waited for this man to arrive and pick me up. But I need not have concerned myself. Paddy was a good looking, pleasant young man about twenty-one years-old, while I, on the other hand, was only seventeen. The lavish meal and elegant surroundings were a bit overwhelming to me, but Paddy was a proper gentleman. I felt comfortable in his presence because he was so easy to talk to that he put me right at ease.

When we danced and I trod on his feet, he assured me it was all right and explained, "Just follow my feet, Beatrice." After an enjoyable evening, he ordered a taxi cab to take me home. He walked me to my door and thanked me for a nice time. I was told he eventually emigrated to Australia.

The legal age in Scotland for marriage was sixteen, and Mom wanted me to "Do well," as she put it. She had high hopes for me and was always thinking ahead for my future. I, on the other hand, was always thinking of getting away. I had already seen a few of our friends married at sixteen, some with babies, and I knew this was not for me, even though I wanted to get out of my overcrowded home. I could not see marrying as an escape, only for the right reason. I was a romantic fool who wanted to be swept off my feet and marry for love.

One of my hobbies was buying records of my latest singing idols. I enjoyed romantic songs, theme music from musical movies, or any others that caught my attention. The rock-and-roll music drove my parents wild, and they did not like it at all. Dad often played Irish records and led me around the kitchen to the tune of a waltz or a highland fling, but he could not comprehend this "rubbish" of rock and roll. Since I had attended Irish step-dancing classes for a short duration when younger, I enjoyed Irish, Scottish, and classical music.

I acquired another pen friend, this time from La Puente, California. His name was George, and he was twenty years old and employed by an airline company. He was at least six-foot tall and very good looking. I enjoyed writing to him and looked forward to receiving his nice letters and cards.

A cookie factory in Hillington, a big industrial estate, was hiring packers, and I applied for a job there. When I was being interviewed, the personnel people were kind to me. I had to have my hair and fingernails checked to ensure I was clean. To my delight I was hired. Since the estate was some distance away from my home, I had to travel by bus to and from work, but the wages were good and the working conditions were excellent. I was taught to pack cookies into boxes as they came around a conveyer-belt machine. Mary and May, the two female supervisors, were nice to me, and I was a conscientious employee. I made lots of friends. Mom liked the fact that I was paid on a Wednesday and that I also received a discount on the chocolate cookies I bought.

One of the girls I worked with was from Ireland, and she told me that the Irish dances were usually held on Friday nights at St. Margaret's in Kinning Park. "What should I do, Ma? How do I act?" I asked her as I got dressed to attend the dance.

"Oh, just act natural, but do not be too anxious if a boy asks you for a dance," she replied.

The hall was quite big and had a fine dance floor. Girls stood on one side and the boys on the opposite. I did not get a dance. "How can I dance if nobody asks me?" I complained to Mom. I kept up enough nerve to keep attending the Friday night dances, and on my third visit I finally was asked to dance.

Occasionally on Saturdays I worked overtime at the cookie factory cleaning the chocolate off of the machinery. My wage increase, plus overtime, meant a lot to me, and I saved money to buy clothes. My sisters accompanied me to Glasgow whenever I went on a spending spree for bargains. We traveled by subway or bus, and when I could afford it, I bought them lunch and a treat afterwards, as we were not accustomed to eating out.

I would plan ahead and save so much money. The anticipation of our Saturday out was a lot of the fun. We didn't always find bargains, but sometimes I'd just have my hair trimmed and then buy fancy writing paper and envelopes. They could choose what they like to eat, followed by dessert or a chocolate bar and lemonade. Some sweet was appreciated by all of us, and I was happy to treat my sisters. They sort of looked to me for support and admired me for being older and, maybe, wiser.

There were two hearing-impaired girls working beside me. One of them was a young woman who attended the dances regularly. Intercom music was played for the employees, and this girl knew if it was a fast or slow melody or song playing. I asked her, "How can you tell when you cannot hear?" She smiled and pointed to the floor—the vibrations!

Mary was an older-woman employee who often trained me for different packing jobs. Everybody liked her because of her sunny nature. She also sang beautifully. Her eyesight had deteriorated, and she was eager to have her eyes operated on. She was a little apprehensive as she left on a leave of absence because she said it was only one-half of a chance of correction, yet she was willing to take it.

A few months later, when the supervisor led Mary through our department, she was blind and walked with the aid of a white walking cane. "Hello, Beatrice," she said, "How are you today?" The lump in my throat almost choked me as I shook her hand, and I could not speak to her. Mary had received the bitter side.

Another friend at the factory was Ina, who lived in the Gorbals District of Glasgow. One time I attended a most enjoyable New Year's Eve party at her home. Her family and friends were wonderful people. Mom forbade me to associate with Ina outside of working hours, Ina had a better home life than I did.

Ina fell in love with an Indian student, and they were planning to elope to the Outer Hibrides of Scotland. We were such good friends that she came to say good-bye to me at my home. Mom refused to let me talk to her. She answered the door and assured Ina that I was not at home. I could hear Ina say, "Beatrice said she would be here!" I was sad that Mom did this to me and my friend.

A few weeks prior to Ina's departure, I remarked to her that I wanted to add blond highlights to my auburn hair, although I knew my parents would not permit it. Ina gave me the instructions, and I waited until my parents left to attend their Monday evening movie. I mixed the formula in an old cup and used a toothbrush to apply it to my hair. After waiting for some time and seeing no results, I retired to bed.

"Oh, my God! What have you done to your hair?" It was 6 AM the following morning and my irate mom called me to rise and get ready for work. Half awake I looked in the mirror to see the entire front of my hair was bleached blond. I was required to wear a turban on my head at my job, so only the front stuck out a tiny bit. At home I was insulted to no end. Mom said I looked like a bun or galice, as well as a cheap and not-nice girl.

I had saved enough money to pay for a trip to Northern Ireland, and Mom, my three sisters, Brother Ed, Cousin Betty, and two girls who were work friends of Mom's, Jean and Heather, accompanied me. Dad preferred to stay at home. Once again, we decided to go visit Mom's Cousin Annie for a change of pace and some fresh air.

The two girls were not used to living on a farm. It was such a hot summer and the girls went out walking wearing their bathing suits. They walked too far and became over-tired, so they hitched a ride back to the cottage in a truck. It so happened that the driver had a bad reputation. Annie was livid with anger when they arrived back, although they assured her that the man was very polite and nice to them.

We were very amused the following day. Apparently the girls awakened in the night and had to urinate, but were afraid to venture outside. They used one of Annie's kitchen basins and were going to empty it in the morning before she awoke. However, Annie was up early as usual and all we heard was her screaming, "Dirty Scotch bitches!" as she tossed the basin and its contents over the ditch and into a field. The basin which they used was the special one she used to make the dough for her bread.

To top it off, who should appear at the cottage that afternoon but the local parish priest. He had heard reports of two girls walking along the countryside half naked and hitching rides from undesirable people. The priest was very nasty and started to reprimand the two girls. "Do not yell at me!" Heather retorted, "I am not even a Catholic. I am a Protestant!"

"Non-Catholics in your house, Annie," declared the good man. "What a crime!" Annie helped out at this priest's house and did his laundry, and she was absolutely mortified by his remarks. But the lassies from Scotland were not even bothered by his insults.

One awfully hot Saturday afternoon I overheard a buzzing noise that came from the men's bedroom. The door was open, so I went in, and I opened the sideboard door. There was the meat that Annie had gotten for our Sunday dinner, sitting on a shelf, and covered with little, fat maggots.

I ran outside to Annie, who was hanging out the laundry. "Annie the meat is covered with small worms!" I told her.

"I am sure you are mistaken, Beatrice," she retorted. She went into the cottage, and I hung out the rest of the laundry.

A little later I returned to the cottage, and Annie said, "What is the matter with you? There is nothing wrong with the meat!" I could not believe my eyes, there was not a sign of anything. The meat was nice and red and clean. Naturally, I refused to eat it on Sunday. Yet, everyone else ate it and did not get sick.

Tony Devlin, the boy I had met on my previous holidays to lovely County Tyrone, visited me almost daily, and he really liked me. I noticed he had grown taller and had the bluest eyes and good looks. We attended a movie in a town called Magherafelt, about five miles from the cottage. I felt achy but happy as I sat on the bar of his bicycle. We shared a chocolate bar and enjoyed the Western movie *Calamity Jane*. He left me off at home and said, "Goodnight," without even kissing me. We also enjoyed his sisters Rosemary and Stella and three of the brothers, Jimmy, Frank, and Wooshy, but it was Tony who came around to visit most of the time. The night before my departure home to Scotland, Tony gently put his arms around me and said that he loved me and gave me a timid kiss. I was overwhelmed. I just put my arms around his neck and said I would write to him.

We enjoyed our holidays very much, but it was time to go home. The bus arrived in Belfast early, which gave us time to buy small gifts for friends. On the previous holiday, when Brother Ed and I had made money from selling our blackberries, we went gift shopping and the bill cost just about all of it. He never forgave me and always reminded me that, "I done him in."

Upon our arrival home to Govan we had a pleasant surprise. Dad had purchased a second-hand car. He also bought a yellow canary named Ricky, that whistled all day long.

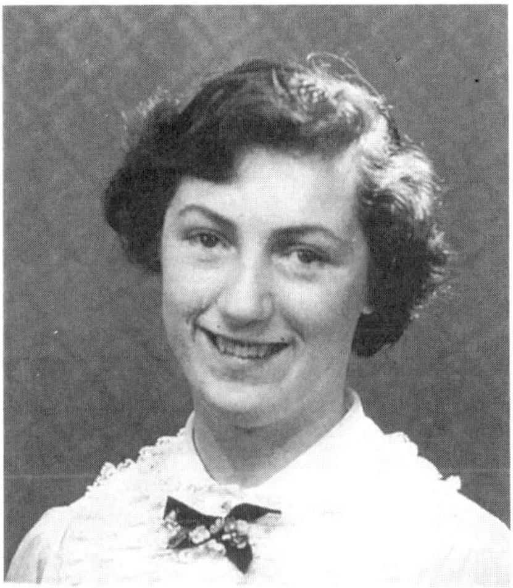

Bridget, age 17

A letter was waiting for me from my American pen friend, George, who lived in LaPuente, California. He was going on holiday to Acapulco, Mexico. Since I attended the movies frequently, he had sent me a year's subscription to a movie magazine and also informed me that a box of glazed fruits was on its way to me. He requested my picture, so I wore my new dress and had one taken. Mom remarked that she would write me a letter everyday if she could put me in such a good mood as when I received letters from George. I never spoke to him since we did not have a telephone, but I lived for his letters, which became longer and friendlier.

I received a pretty, white-lace blouse and slip that he had his sister pick out and send to me, along with lovely cards. The letters and cards were first signed, "Your friend." Then this changed to, "My dear friend." Finally George got up the nerve to write, "All my love." My parents became concerned, and Mom questioned, "How can he love you when he has not met you or does not even know you?"

I said, "Ma, I sent him my picture."

She replied, "Beatrice, pictures are very flattering. If he sees you in person, he may not even like you." I was so depressed by this remark that I stopped writing to him, and I did not answer any of his letters. Eventually his letters stopped coming.

My job was going well, and I enjoyed working. The young man who delivered coal to us weekly asked me on a date, and I accepted. I knew him well enough because when he returned on Friday's to collect the money we were all at home and if I did not answer the door, he asked for me specially. We both enjoyed cycling and he said he would meet me on Sunday. Sure enough he appeared at my door and he was all cleaned up wearing a dark suit, a nice shirt, and a tie and his shoes were polished. We went to his home in Clydebank and I met his family and they had dinner waiting for us. I knew I wanted to emigrate to America and it would be unfair to take advantage of him because he liked me and I never went on any more dates. We remained friends.

My parents were annoyed because I had been saying this for years. Finally they told me, "Forget this nonsense talk. We have no relatives in the U.S. to claim or sponsor you, Beatrice." But I knew I was going someday, no matter what they said. I believed and felt it in my heart always.

One Monday night while I was reading the newspaper I came across an article regarding "Men's Opinion of the Perfect Woman." It said, "Come on, girls! Write to us, giving your opinion of the perfect man." I wrote, "My idea of the perfect man. He must be clean living, fond of walking, biking, dancing, reading, travel, and movies." I mailed the letter and forgot about it. The following week my letter appeared on the inside cover of the local newspaper, and I was bombarded with letters from men saying, "I am the one for you." My parents were very upset with me, and I was advised not to answer any of them.

On weekends, Dad often drove all of us to one of the many lovely seaside resorts within hours of our home. He was not a good driver. If another car passed us, he had to catch up with it. He even passed going up hills! We had many narrow escapes.

When we went to Brassy in Ayrshire, Dad drove on the beach. The tide was coming in, and the car got stuck in the sand. We became hysterical and had to get out and push it clear. He just laughed, because he knew the tide better than we did, since he had lived near the sea in Ireland.

Televisions were becoming popular, and I wanted my parents to rent a set. Dad said if Mom or I attempted to get one, he would throw it out of our kitchen window. Eventually he relented, and he enjoyed watching it more than any of us!

Ed graduated from high school and entered Stephens Shipyard's training program as a five-year apprentice to become a caulker-burner welder. My brother enjoyed his job training at the shipyard. He joined the boxing club there and won a medal in amateur boxing. We were very proud of him and realized how good he really was when he proved this to us one Saturday morning.

We all overslept, and Dad came into our bedroom and threw a piece of stale, hard bread at my brother. Ed awoke startled as it hit him in the face. Up he jumped out of his bed and gave Dad such a punch that he landed outside our bedroom door flat on his back. Dad was so surprised, but only his pride was hurt. However, he never pushed my brother around after this incident, especially after Ed said, "There is more where that came from!"

My sister Rose blossomed into a lovely girl with a good figure, her green eyes, and jet black hair with a widow's peak. She wore it up in a roll at the back and really looked elegant. Dad seemed to be upset with her good looks and made nasty remarks, "Why can't you be like your sister Beatrice?" Dad said that her bust resembled a cow's udder–she was then maybe a size-thirty-six bra. I was very thin and small busted and wished I could look more like my sister Rose! I never envied her. I loved her. She was my pal.

Violet, my youngest sister, was inclined to stay outdoors. To be certain that none of us tenement children wandered away from our own street or stayed out too late, we were warned from an early age about the boogey man. He would chase after children who did not come home when their parents requested them. We never questioned our parents about this boogey man or even what he looked like, because we were scared out of our wits. We realized he must be a very evil, bad person.

We were also assured that if any child picked at her nose, it would fall off just like Johnny Boggins' nose.

"Who is Johnny Boggins?" we asked Dad.

"Well," he explained, "Johnny was a man who was forever picking his nose, and finally his nose fell off!" Johnny was a figure of imagination, and Dad's parents in Ireland probably said the same to him when he was a boy.

Rose and I went on a two-week cycling trip to Sligo. Granda no longer stayed at his farm, and only my uncle Jimmy remained there, and he never married. Granda was getting old and feeble and was now living at Cousin Nancy's home. She was married now and living on a farm in Dromore with her husband and sweetheart, Tom Feeney. They were expecting their first child.

Poor Granda. It broke my heart to see him so child like. He did not even recognize me. I sat beside him at the kitchen table as he ate his soft-boiled egg and watched it drip down his chin onto his light beard. He drooled and tried to feed himself as best as he could. Cousin Nancy was very kind to him and encouraged him, "Eat up your egg and bread, Da."

Rose and I stayed with the Thorntons, Bea and John, who had been good friends of my grandparents. They were childless and enjoyed having us staying at their home. Their cottage had two bedrooms and was similar to most of the homes at that time. The Thornton's were a close and happy couple, and they introduced us to the neighbor children around our age. We enjoyed going to the bog with them and helping to toss the sods of turf into a truck. We also saw many donkey-drawn carts filled with turf and lots of people cutting the turf into sods with a spade. It was so peaceful and quiet at the bog, and the fresh air smelled good.

My sister and I cycled all over the place and visited the relatives. We also visited Winny and Pat Flannery, and they were very pleased to see us. They remarked that I was still a grand girl and loved meeting Rose. Pat had his first set of dentures and was very proud of his new teeth; he smiled a lot. Next stop was Tommy Ryan and his aunt, Mrs. Green. Tom was married now and we met his gracious wife, Greta, who was a good farmer like Tom. Mrs. Green had died, and I missed seeing her again. Uncle Danny was married, and his wife, Agnes, made us very welcome. Although they married late in life, it seemed like a very happy marriage. Since they lived near Dunmoran Strand, we went for a stroll on the beach and also had a swim in the water.

We thoroughly enjoyed our holidays. As Rose and I said our good-byes to the relatives and friends, we were a little saddened to be leaving Ireland, yet happy to be returning home to our family in Scotland.

I went back to my job at the cookie factory, which should have been enjoyable to me. However, an older-woman employee, who was apparently hooked on gambling, made my life miserable, as she became very moody and nasty to me. So when a vacancy at the furniture factory where Mom worked became available, I applied for the job.

To my delight, I was hired. My job was as an apprentice sewer, and I was trained to hand sew cushions and also parts of covers on sofas and chairs. This was done with a special, curved needle. The needle was tough on the fingers, but after a short time the skin on my fingers became rough and callused, and it did not hurt anymore. My job paid better wages than I received at the cookie factory, and I usually worked overtime until 8 PM on Tuesdays.

Since I already knew a few of the other employees who were Mom's friends, it was pleasant to be employed there. One in particular whom I truly admired was Joe Mishel, a Polish man. He was an upholsterer, but had been a saddle maker in his native Poland. He could make beautiful, leather handbags, wallets, and such. His wife, Stasha, was a lovely woman—Russian and Jewish, I believe—and she was learning to speak English.

Joe, his first wife, and their son were prisoners at Auschwitz, the German prison camp. His wife and son died there, and miraculously he managed to escape along with a few others. Stasha happened to be one of them. Stasha showed my mom her awful wounds, where her stomach had been bayoneted to such an extent that she would never be able to bear children. She loved children and was employed in Glasgow at a children's home.

Mom always tried to keep Saturday afternoons special for Dad. She cooked one of his favorite meals, which was steak, onions, potatoes, and a vegetable. The table would be set with a white-linen table cloth for him alone. He came home around 3 PM, and she had his dinner waiting. Sometimes he was so pleasant and happy, even singing. At other times he was so grouchy and nasty. Many times I observed that as Mom placed his dinner on the table, he would wait until everything was completed and then, in a fit of anger for no good reason that we were aware of, he would grab a corner of the tablecloth, and in a quick pull, everything would fall onto the floor, without anything spilling on him.

We had an old-fashioned bureau in the kitchen, and it had a large mirror which we all used. One Saturday afternoon as I was getting ready to go out shopping, I was standing in front of the mirror combing my hair. Dad was in a nasty mood and making sarcastic remarks, "You are too conceited for your own good."

I remarked, "Eat your dinner, Da." Out of the corner of my eye, I happened to see him getting ready to pull the tablecloth.

I spun around and removed his plate of food, saying, "I will save you the trouble of tossing your meal on the floor, Da." I threw the food all over him. He was in shock! As I ran out of the door, I overheard him say to Mom, "Rosetta, Rosetta! Did you see what that one done to me?" I believe Mom was in shock, and they had to clean it up themselves because I ran out the door so fast. However, this put an end to Saturday dinner being thrown on the floor.

One of the young men at work was an upholsterer, and he worked on the wooden frames of the sofas and chairs that came from the wood shop. His name was Archie, and he and I became friends and dated occasionally. He lived near my home and whenever he was on his way to meet me, I could see him from our kitchen window. He always dressed so nicely and usually carried a big box of chocolate candy for me. Of course, Dad did not approve of this fine man because he was not of the Catholic faith. He said I was forbidden to date him, but I refused to listen because Archie treated me with the utmost devotion and respect. I sometimes ran into him with my hair in rollers and pin curls.

On one occasion, a rainy winter's night, I ran out of my home in tears because Dad was so drunk and nasty. I was walking along the road outside of the park and did not see Archie until I bumped into him. He put his arm around my shoulder to console me and escorted me to the local cafe for a soda and a talk before taking me to my home.

In good weather we could take a nice train ride to Troon or Ayr, two of the many lovely resorts in Scotland. When the carnival came to Glasgow Green, we traveled there by bus. We had fun trying our luck at the many booths. One time I won two goldfish, which they placed in a plastic bag filled with water to take home. On returning home, I left them on the kitchen sink overnight. When I awakened the next morning, the water had run out overnight, and to my dismay, the fish were laying there dead. I cried my eyes out. Dad said, "Do not be so childish, they are only goldfish!" But I felt guilty, as if I had killed them.

There was a pleasant man who worked in the woodshop as a carpenter, and he dated me a few times. Ma did not approve of him because he was at least eight years older than me and she felt he was too wise for me. His name was Dave. On our first date, he came to meet me to escort me to the movies at the Lyceum, and he suggested we stop at the Brechin bar for a drink. I wanted to impress him, so I agreed. I looked pretty in my new winter coat. The bar was crowded with men, and we went upstairs to the nicely-decorated lounge bar, and sat at one of the many tables that were occupied with mostly couples.

Dave asked me, "Bea, what do you want? Do you want a drink?"

I replied, "What have they got?"

He said, "How about gin and orange juice?"

And I agreed. I did not feel at ease because I knew I should not be there, but I figured my parents would never know. The place was warm and I was thirsty and promptly swallowed down the first drink. My date ordered a second drink for me, which was also gone in no time. Half way through my third drink, I started feeling sick, so I excused myself, "I have to go powder my nose," which was what ladies were supposed to say.

When I entered the ladies' room I could scarcely see my face in the mirror and vomited in the wash basin. I managed to clean out the sink and rinse my mouth. I went back to the table, and we left soon afterwards to attend the movie. As we were walking along the road, I suddenly became violently sick and vomited at the edge of the sidewalk. My poor date never realized I had never drank liquor before. I was worried my new coat would become soiled.

In the movies my date began caressing my leg. I said, "What do you think you're doing?"

He replied, "I like to touch the nylon stocking."

I became angry and said, "Stop it or I will tell my dad, and he will kill you!"

A few weeks passed by, and one evening Mom arrived home very angry from an evening out. Apparently she had met a neighbor woman, who said, "Oh, Mrs. Dowd, I saw your lassie a few weeks ago. She was vomiting out on Govan road, and I never felt so sorry for anyone in my entire life."

Mom replied hotly, "Not my girl. Bea would never set foot inside a bar or drink liquor."

The neighbor described what I was wearing that night, and it was my new, blue coat with the fox-fur trim that gave me away. Dad was so shocked he did not utter a word.

I went on two more dates with Dave, but since he liked to drink to excess I lost interest in him. Our last date was when he invited me to come to his home and watch television. When I arrived, his mother met me at the door wearing her coat and hat. She said, "I am going to play bingo, enjoy yourself."

Dave invited me to sit next to him on the sofa, but I became afraid for some reason so I said, "I am sorry, Dave. I suddenly feel sick and I have to leave." I ran home to my mom. She assured me I had done the right thing. She was still annoyed with me because I had arrived home from our last date with a big hickey on my neck. I had been so ashamed that I wore my high-necked blouse for almost a week so my parents would not see it. Mom said, "I hope you are not going out on any more dates with that vampire!"

I also dated a nice Irish man I had met while I was employed at the cookie factory. His name was John, and he was a construction worker. My friend and I used to walk around on our dinner break at noon, and John took a real shine to me and asked me out on dates. He did not drink but enjoyed smoking cigarettes. Dad called him a "teetotaler," as he did not particularly care for men who did not drink alcoholic beverages.

One Christmas John gave my dad a bottle of whisky. When we arrived home after our date, Dad was blind drunk in bed, seeing bottles of whisky hanging on the ceiling and saying to my date, "You have my blessings if you want to marry my daughter." Needless to say I was very embarrassed.

John wanted to take me to meet his newly-married friend, so I said to Mom, "I want to look older, more worldly, stylish, and sophisticated." I borrowed her big, navy blue picture hat, handbag, and her treasured fox fur that Dad had purchased for her when they were newly married and he had won money at horse racing. This was a real fox fur, complete with a tail, paws, and glass eyes. As I sat on the crowded subway, people looked at me and smiled, and I thought to myself, "They think that I am beautiful." I really believed that I did look beautiful. When John met me, he nearly had a fit. "Surely you do not expect me to take you anywhere dressed like that?" So I became angry and got a return ticket and went home. He was a good person but we were not meant for each other, as we had little in common. He was older and ready to settle down, whereas I was ready to move on with my life.

I remember when stiletto-heeled shoes were fashionable, and I was thrilled to bits with my first pair. They were navy blue with white dots on the front of the pointed toes. Dad remarked, "Pet, sure now, you could kick the eyes out of a sparrow with those shoes." My feelings were hurt and even Ricky, the yellow canary, seemed to be singing, "Your shoes are ugly; yes, they are ugly."

It was so much fun to be able to buy clothes, and I searched for bargains at the sales. One January there was a sale at a very good quality clothing store. I had spotted a red winter coat on the mannequin in the window, and upon inquiring, I discovered it was my size. Mom did not think I would ever get out of my warm bed on a freezing Saturday morning to stand in line until the store opened at 9 AM. But, since I was first in line, I bought the coat. As I pranced around our kitchen to model it for my family, Mom repeated her usual saying: "Health to wear it, strength to tear it and money to buy another."

I never had any pretty underwear growing up. What we had to wear were always dark brown or navy blue, cotton, long-legged, elastic knickers. At this age I took more interest in my appearance, and now I was able to afford lingerie and a tiny bottle of perfume, and I delighted in being feminine and well groomed. I took more interest in my appearance, but we were always clean because from an early age, my ma was firm that we always washed our hands, and she often quoted, "Cleanliness is next to godliness."

My brother Ed was self-conscious because he thought he was too thin and his friends teased him. He sent away for a keep-fit-and-exercise book. When it arrived in the mail, he was very serious and studious about the exercises in the book. Every morning the two windows of our bedroom were opened wide because Ed had to do his breathing exercises and us four sisters would be so cold and shivery. Well, it paid off. My dear brother became a fine, built, handsome young man.

When I was eighteen years old, my sister Patricia, who was twelve, graduated to high school. She had grown up into a lovely girl with delicate and refined good looks and was like brother Ed when it came to being studious. She made it to St. Gerald's High School too. I was so proud of Patricia, and I felt a pang of guilt whenever I thought of the many teasing and smacking episodes I gave to her when she was younger and whiny. It had not occurred to me that she missed Mom so badly, especially when Mom had worked evenings at the shipyard or had to work late at the furniture factory. Being the middle child was tough on her. I tried to make it up to her as we got older, as I really loved my three sisters and my brother. I truly believe our living conditions caused a lot of our problems.

The people I worked with at the furniture factory were happy and pleasant to be with. Sylvia Ross and I went to the Locarno Ballroom and Barrowland, and she taught me some of the dances. Isa Gaye introduced me to her friends, as I joined them for a night of old-time dancing. I learned the polka and military two-step dance, as well as a modern waltz.

We also had ladies' night out. First we ate dinner at a nice restaurant and afterwards we attended a show at a theater in Glasgow. Mary Glasgow often loaned me dresses for special occasions. We also had a holiday savings club at work, and we made weekly deposits to ensure that we employees had money to plan our yearly holidays.

My sisters Rose and Violet accompanied me for two-week holiday to Stornoway, which is the capital of the Isle of Lewis in the Outer Hebrides of Scotland. I wanted to explore my own country for a change. The people there were friendly, and I liked them immensely. Many of them were born in Glasgow of highland parents, while others had traveled to the mainland to find employment or to attend the Glasgow University to study to become doctors and nurses at our excellent hospitals.

I had written to the town-hall tourist department of Stornoway, inquiring as to guest-house rental accommodations, and I chose one about half a mile from the town. We had a very enjoyable trip by train and boat and arrived at our destination to find the lady and her husband waiting for us. They escorted us to their guest house and made us welcome. Our bedroom had three comfortable beds and a white, lamb's-wool rug on the floor, which we looked at and thought of the poor lamb it must have belonged to before it was made into a rug. We were fed delicious sandwiches before retiring to bed. The next morning we awakened to the aroma of bacon and sausages cooking for our breakfast. We were the only guests, and since the couple who owned the guest house grew their own vegetables and caught their own fish, they fed us well.

Stornoway was a lovely place, and my sisters and I enjoyed many long walks along the shore and throughout the town, where we observed the spinning and weaving of sweaters and Harris tweed by the local people. At one crofter's cottage, we stopped to chat to the owners. Their son Roddy and his friend Sandy befriended us and took us to see a movie.

Sandy was six feet tall and had dark hair. We went on long, friendly walks, but we were just talking—no kissing, no nothing. Roddy was blonder with blue eyes, and there was no romance there either. We were just good friends and kept in touch. Afterwards Roddy visited us in Glasgow.

We discovered that on Sundays no pleasurable activities—such as playing the radio or dancing—were allowed, and it was strictly observed. We were surprised to find that there was no Catholic church in Stornoway, but only a priest who came ashore once a month to say mass. The first Sunday we went walking and met a minister, who was indignant to find us out walking and laughing. When he inquired why we were not attending church, we replied, "Build us one and we'll attend. We're Catholics."

While gazing out the window one day, I spied the mailman talking to the lady of the house in Gaelic. When she made the sign of the cross and blessed herself while looking up toward our bedroom window, I realized she was discussing us. She was obviously unhappy having Catholics living under her roof. As she had informed us to ring the tiny bell that was on the dining room table if we required anything more to eat or drink, naturally we rang the bell and kept her hopping after this episode with the mailman.

The landlady had a very nice daughter who was employed as a nurse in Glasgow, and she came to visit while we were there. Her fiancé had a car, and they drove us around the island and were very kind to us. When our two-week holiday ended the two young men, Sandy and Roddy, came to the door to see us off, and they presented us with a big, wooden box of smoked fish. I left them our home address and assured them of a warm welcome if they ever decided to pay a visit to Glasgow.

We arrived home in Govan to find Dad in his usual, pouty mood. He accused us of being selfish, going off on our holidays and leaving him all alone with nobody to take care of him. Mom knew before we left that she was going into the hospital for a repair operation, yet she had chosen not to tell us as she felt this would spoil our holidays. Patricia and Brother Ed were staying with friends. We were shocked to arrive home and find no mother waiting for us. She always remarked later how she got a big kick out of seeing the three of us running down the hospital ward yelling, "Ma! Ma! Are you all right?" She returned home shortly afterwards.

The employees at my work were planning a September weekend trip to Blackpool, in the north of England, to see the illumination lights. Mom decided to send Rose and me, and we were looking forward to the trip. Since it was an overnight trip, the bus was to leave at 10 PM. As we sat on the bus as it was about to leave, Rose and I were saying, "Thank goodness, Dad did not show up to see us off!" The driver was just closing the doors, and who appeared but our father, a bit intoxicated. "Where are my two girls? I must say good-bye to them!" he exclaimed. Rose and I tried to hide low in our seats. He had a little buzz on him, so he stepped aboard and walked towards us. He wished us a safe journey and reminded us to be sure to attend mass on Sunday.

Rose, 14, and Bridget, 18, in Blackpool, England.

We arrived in Blackpool early the following morning. We were disappointed to find that our guest house had overbooked, and so we were put in the basement. The iron beds were placed together and it was difficult to sleep. From the end of August to early November, the Blackpool Illuminations are a sight to behold. Lights shape out the faces of famous movie stars and animals, and all sorts of shapes shine from the top of every pole. It was a breathtaking delight to see the lovely light display on every pole.

The following spring I was sitting at home about 6 PM just soaking my feet in a pail of water. Who appeared at our door but Roddy, one of the men we had met while on holiday on the Isle of Lewis. He was working aboard a whaling ship. My family welcomed him and he visited every few weeks, usually carrying wads of money. I really only liked him as a friend, and I tried to discourage his visits, but to no avail. I made excuses not to go out on dates with him. I told him, "I have to mind my three sisters and my brother Ed." Roddy insisted that was no problem, and he escorted all five of us by bus to Glasgow to see the latest movie, bought us all candy and ice cream and soda and took us back home. He stayed at the sailors' hotel when he was ashore in Glasgow. This fine man remained my friend, and I could not lose him no matter how I tried. He always showed up! As Mom remarked, "See what happens when you give your address to strangers."

My job was going well at the furniture factory, but I did not enjoy working with my mom. Any little thing I did wrong at work, she would go home in the evening and tell Dad.

Tony Cauley asked me for a date, and we went to the movies together. He never requested a second date, so I figured he did not find me attractive enough. Since I knew him very well only as a good friend, I really think the date was Dad's idea anyway. Tony's aunt in Philadelphia sponsored him, and as he left for a new life in America, he cried as he bade us all good-bye. Tony wrote to my parents, but he was eventually called to join the army and seldom wrote afterwards.

In 1959, my sister Rose graduated from school at the age of fifteen. She was employed as an usherette at the Vogue Cinema. My parents were very proud of her.

CHAPTER 6

Bridget Looks Ahead To America

A few evenings a week I visited our local library, where I read books about America. Around this time, Dad was seriously thinking of immigrating to Australia. He even had an interview with the Australian Consulate in Glasgow, who told Dad they wanted complete families only. They offered to pay our fares, put us up in good accommodations in a big house with other Scottish people, and offered Dad plenty of work choices, which were plentiful in Australia. However, Dad wanted to go on his own first, to see what it was like, and then send for all of us. Needless to say, we did not go to Australia.

One night while reading the local newspaper, I came across an advertisement where a London agency was offering child care and nanny jobs in America. The price was ten pounds in British money. The requirements for any girl who applied was to be of good character and in good health, and she had to supply her picture, plus three references.

Mom did her utmost to discourage me, even going so far as to pay a visit to our parish priest. To my surprise, Father McElholm told her, "Let the girl go, if she has her heart set on it."

I became very upset because my parents were so reluctant to let me go. Our family doctor suggested I have a change of scenery and a mild sedative to relax me. William Crighton, my work manager, agreed to give me two weeks leave of absence. And off I went to County Tyrone in Northern Ireland. I had written to Dorothy and Joe Devlin, and they invited me to come over on holiday. They were pleased to have me stay with them. Rosemary was especially pleased as we were the same age, and I attended dances with her and her cousins. Tony avoided me like the plague, since he was now engaged to be married.

A neighbor of the Devlins, an older lady who lived in a big house along with her nephew, very kindly drove me in their car to attend a movie. I liked the nephew, except he was rather shy and hardly uttered a word.

The Devlins were growing up, and they enjoyed my efforts to dance the Irish jig or sing songs to them. Rosemary was planning on going to England to join her fiancé, and her mother did not like the idea of her leaving home one bit. Jimmy, Wooshy, and Stella were always busy working, as were their parents. After two weeks of holiday, I was sad as I bade them good-bye and told them I was going to America.

When I returned home to Scotland, the doctor vaccinated me for smallpox in preparation of my trip to America. There was nothing to it, just a little scrape on my upper left arm. Two weeks later my neck felt achy and stiff, and I could hardly turn my head. It was difficult to work because I felt so sick, and my left arm was all red and sore. Mom assured me it was only a cold that I had because I was forever washing myself and shampooing my hair and going to bed with wet hair.

By Christmas I could not get up out of my bed. My parents sent for the doctor, and he had to make a house call. The glands of my neck and arm pits were so swollen that I required double doses of penicillin. He was very concerned, and I overheard him telling my parents that if I had contracted small pox I would have died!

The London Agency also requested a copy of my birth certificate, and so Mom sent for it. I recall the evening that I arrived home from work with Mom, and there was a letter waiting for me—my birth certificate. I opened it and read it, and then I exclaimed, "Ma! Da! There must be some mistake!"

My parents were sitting on their chairs, reading the evening newspaper and not paying any attention to me or so it seemed. I said, "How can this be? My birth certificate states that you were married in December 1939, and I was born in April 1940, four months later." As I looked up, I was so saddened to see my parents' faces almost purple, heads buried in the newspaper. Not until that very moment did I realize that I had embarrassed them. I looked at my mother and thought, "My poor ma, what a price you have paid."

The agency offered me a promising position as a nanny for a family with two children in New Jersey. Shortly afterwards, I received a very nice letter from the lady. She explained that she and her husband were the parents of a little girl and boy and she had enclosed their pictures. The couple was a handsome pair, and the children were about two years old and four years old. The lady said her husband was a lawyer, and they were expecting another child. Hopefully they could arrange for my arrival to America before the new baby's birth. She also explained that she and her husband had chosen me after going through loads of other applicants.

Needless to say, I was surprised and delighted that such a well-to-do family in far-off America had thought me good enough to join their family. They assured me that I would be treated like a member of the family while living at their split-level, ranch home. My work friends were very pleased for me, although Archie was not too happy at the idea of my leaving home.

Weeks went by with no more word of when I would be immigrating. I had acquired all the necessary papers and my passport. One day I arrived home around dinnertime, and there was a letter waiting for me from the couple in New Jersey: "So sorry, we could not wait for you and had to engage someone else." I was heartbroken and very embarrassed, as I had told everyone I knew, "I will be off soon to America!"

The London Agency offered me another job at a New York Hospital to train as a nursing technician, and I was hopeful to become a nurse someday. I told my parents, "I do not think I could ever become a nurse." Mom got all excited, "Oh, Beatrice, just think—a nurse in the family! Wouldn't that be wonderful?"

Dad said, "Beatrice, you are a good-hearted girl. Do you remember not too long ago when we went to visit old Joe at the geriatric building of the hospital?" Did I ever remember! It was truly an awful experience for me. We had lost track of Joe, and Dad had managed to locate him. He and I drove to the hospital to visit him.

Joe was in a big ward along with other men. He was laying in bed naked and so thin I could see his bones, yet he was very clean, as was his bed linen. He was squirming about mumbling to himself, more like an animal than a person, I thought. He had lost his mind. As I gazed at this old man who had become such a part of my childhood, I was overcome with emotion, and I became almost hysterical. One of our neighbors who worked there escorted me out of the building. After consoling me, Dad drove me to visit his brother, my uncle John, who lived about ten minutes from the hospital. Aunt Annie was home and she made us tea.

The job in America required a one-year, signed contract, and I accepted the job offer in New York. Afterwards I received literature in the mail telling me about, "The New World—America." The hospital would sponsor me and pay my fare, which would be deducted off my wages in installments every pay period. I would live in a dormitory of the hospital.

I had a choice of traveling by sea or air, and I choose to travel by sea on the *Queen Mary*. My co-workers presented me with a gift of luggage. My parents gave me a farewell party where I received many

Bridget's Farewell party. (First row) John McCabe, Bridget, and Rose. (Second row) Ma, Da, Aunt Maggy, and Uncle Robert. (Third row) Violet, Patsy, and Isabel Campbell.

gifts such as a travel clock and my very first wrist watch. Uncle Robert and Aunt Maggy gave me a gold locket.

One of Mom's older-woman friends read my fortune from the left-over tea leaves in my cup. She said, "I can see you are going across water." What a laugh, since I had chosen to sail to America on a beautiful ship which had been built in Scotland! Everyone was so happy for me. Aunt Mary sang songs for me in her lovely, soprano voice, and Margaret joined her mom in singing along. We all sang the old tunes and the new songs of the day. I was so overjoyed and preoccupied with my trip that it had not occurred to me that Archie was unhappy about my leaving.

All my dear relatives gave me gifts and took pictures. Mom bought me a new coat. Margaret and James Harte gave me money, as did Lizzy and Donny Maxwell, Aunt Mary and Uncle Larry, and my friend Margaret. Our neighbor, Mary Burnett, gave me rosary beads to keep me safe on my travels.

Bridget's Farewell Party. Bridget with Margaret and "Aunt Mary" McNally.

Almost the last thing I did was go to the bank to withdraw the one-hundred-pounds sterling that my dad had deposited for me from his settlement almost six years previous. To my dismay, there was less than half the amount left! Every weekend since my father had given me this gift, I had been reminded of it so much that I hated it and felt it was never really mine. Apparently my mother had been withdrawing from it, and I approached her. I cried, "Oh Ma, what if Da finds out?" She became furious and said, "Beatrice, that hundred pounds should have been mine, not yours."

The evening finally arrived for my departure. We had more pictures taken, and my parents even had theirs taken, with Dad actually putting his arm around my mom's shoulders. In all my years growing up, this was the first sign of affection I had ever seen. They never held hands or kissed, or showed each other any kind of affection. I often heard their voices in the night, so they must have had a special time just for each other, but they did not show this side to the public.

The big, black taxi arrived to take me and my family to the train station. I was to travel overnight to England and stay at Aunt Nora, Uncle Bill and Cousin Sandra's home in Southampton for one day, as the *Queen Mary* was docked there. My family was so sad at my departure, and Mom and Dad were heartbroken. Not until that very moment did I realize they loved me in their own way. I thought, "Too late! Too late! I am out of here!" as I waved happily from the window of the train. Edward, Rose, Patricia, and Violet were dressed so well and looked all grown up. "Where did the years go?" I thought as they faded from view.

I had a bunk bed on the train but I could not sleep very well for excitement. I arrived in London the following morning and caught another train to Southampton. My relatives were there to greet me and escort me to their home. Cousin Sandra had grown up into a lovely girl, and I was made very welcome. We talked and laughed about all the old times, years previously, when they had visited in Govan.

Bridget boards the Queen Mary .

The next morning Aunt Nora, Uncle Bill, and Cousin Sandra took me to the dock where I had to board the *Queen Mary* overnight. The ship was set to sail the next morning, and they assured me that they would be back to wave me good-bye. Although the *Queen Mary*, like all the other queen ships, had been built in Scotland at a shipyard not far from my home, I had never actually seen any of them close-up.

The *Queen Mary* was a wonderful sight to behold, and as I stepped aboard, I wondered, "How can this magnificent ocean liner stay afloat in the sea?"